# Create The
# BEST LIFE EVER
## Real Life Stories to Get Inspired

### Taylor Wells

# What Everyone Is Talking About

"Taylor embraces what she teaches with a great heart and her whole being. She is a living example of the power of intention."

- Rolf Gates, Teacher and Author

"Whenever I need an energy boost, a shot of enthusiasm or a reality check, it's Taylor I turn to. Within minutes of spending time with Taylor, I feel renewed, refreshed and back in my power. I'm so happy that she has put her experiences about conscious choice and reality creation into this book so that more people can be touched by her magic fairy dust."

- Alissa Cohen, Author

"Taylor is an absolute inspiration - such a *shining* example of an empowered woman loving her flow and helping others to shine too. I feel Taylor is an ideal role model for busy women in this time of fast-paced lifestyles; she really is a living 'Super-Mom,' loving, positive, healthy, giving, experienced, living her truth and loving it and this book shows how *you* can create the same kind of life for yourself—I love it. Thank you Taylor for being willing to shine so brightly and encouraging other women to do the same —you are a gift to us all."

- Angela Stokes-Monarch, Author

"You don't have to be a yoga practitioner, a raw foodist, a mom, or super in anyway to appreciate Taylor Wells' exuberant and optimistic message. Even a happily childless confirmed cynic and committed skeptic like me had a great time reading her book and (secretly) took away a lot of tips for life with a more productive and positive outlook."

- Stephen McCauley, Author

"Create The Best Life Ever" is a must read for any mom, dad or person really, kids or no kids! Taylor's heart-felt, heart-led, heart-warming and heart-tugging stories and insights are so profound and moving. Her experiences and lust for life are infectious and while reading her stories and her guidance, you feel as if she is your own personal cheerleader. She not only believes that you can have the best life ever, but wants it more for you than she does for herself. Want the best life ever? Begin by reading this book."

- Adrienne Martin, Lic. Ac., Health Educator, and Author

"What a wonderful gift Taylor has created and shared with all of us. Foods you love without restriction, yoga, positive thinking and gratitude all working together; who could ask for more? Taylor's shining light comes right out through the pages and warms my heart. I am sure it will warm the hearts of all who read it.

- Brenda Cobb, Founder Living Foods Institute and Author


"Well done, Taylor, on such a great achievement! Your enthusiasm is contagious - your energy pops off the page and inspires transformation!"

- Natalia Rose, Author


"Taylor Wells artfully expresses the beauty found within delicate choices we face in our day-to-day lives in this uplifting, refreshing, and energetic book. I first began reading it during a particularly challenging afternoon and her words provided the light and guidance I needed. You will love this book and be entertained, motivated, and most grateful for her generosity in sharing some of life's most valuable lessons."

- Matthew Kenney, Chef and Author


"Taylor takes readers on a heartfelt journey that inspires one to choose the highest path for health, harmony and evolution."

- Brigitte Mars, Author


"I loved this book. I found Taylor's book fascinating and inspiring. My personal belief is to not settle for mediocrity but strive to be the most that we can be. I like what Taylor says about making each day the best day ever. Three words that best describe Taylors' book are positive, motivational, and enlightening. Read it if you want a better life."

- Fred Bisci, Author


"Brace yourself! This is not just a book—it is an experience. Taylor invites readers along on her path, allowing us to witness her constant practice of presence. She powerfully illustrates that presence is not a fixed state but rather a choice to be made in each moment. The simple wisdom in this book inspires us to fulfill our birthright and live THE BEST LIFE EVER."

- Venus Taylor, Author

First Edition
Designed by Liz Comperchio

Worldwide Distribution by Prana Publications
Printed in China

The Library of Congress has cataloged this edition as follows:
Wells, Taylor.
Create the best life ever: real life stories to get inspired
Catalog Card Number: 2012910162

ISBN 978-0-9857084-0-5

For Dakota, Madison,
Montana, Philippe,
Phoenix, and Sage

# Gratitude

*"Gratitude is the open door to abundance."*
*- Yogi Bhajan*

I'm a big believer in gratitude. In fact, I do my best to maintain a constant vibration of appreciation through the moments that make up my days and weave the fabric of my life. I am grateful for so many things.

An infinite amount of gratitude to Philippe, my soul mate, life partner, spiritual partner, husband, and partner in many adventures. Your love, support, faith, sense of humor, wit, and never-ending belief in me, my Spirit, and my adventures have made this book a reality. I love you now and always.

A big shout out of gratitude to my five children, Madison, Sage, Phoenix, Dakota, and Montana. As I say repeatedly in my writing and to you on our many fun and exciting adventures, you are my biggest teachers and your mere existence brings me great joy and envelops me with love. Not because of what you do but because of who you are. How did I get so lucky to get you as my children? I love you dearly. Always remember, you can be, do, and have anything that you want. If you believe and follow your joy.

Much gratitude to Liz Comperchio, my graphic designer extraordinaire, who helped make creating this book a joy, all on yoga trade. And thank you to the yogi proof readers and editors extraordinaire, with a big shout out to Austin Lin who proofread and edited twice, both before and after the big re-write. Kristin Caforio, Amanda Califano, Emily Griffin, Ray Mucci, Ossi Raveh, and Beth Toomey, thank you for being our Prana Power Yoga Studio Coordinators Extraordinaires and helping us spread the light and the Prana. Mandy Schwartz, much gratitude for all you do to help me disseminate my words to so many, and for your help spreading the Prana and the light. Joe Dwinell and Jorie Mark, thank you for being the best Managing Editors ever and helping me to reach many people. David Zucker, thank you for having an open mind, an open heart, and an amazing marketing sense.

*I am grateful for so many things.*

To all of my readers of my Best Life Ever blogs, Super-mom.com, and Momonomics, much gratitude for your time, words, wisdom, thoughts, questions, and support.

Much gratitude to all of our students at Prana Power Yoga for your never-ending dedication to your practice, which is making this world a better place, one asana at a time. I bow to you and your intention and grace. Thank you for reading my blogs and this book.

To my dedicated and amazing "tribe" of 4:30 am yoga practitioners who show up every single morning to practice with me in the predawn hours at Prana Power Yoga Newton. The Universe guided me to teach a predawn class daily, and I now know why.

I am grateful for all of our family at Prana Power Yoga—teachers and volunteers (too many to list). Thank you for helping Philippe and me spread the light, joy, and Prana of Prana Power Yoga to so many people. What you do matters.

To my dear friends and soul sisters, Alissa Cohen, Yola Cobert, Deb Cronin, Sara Foley, Judy Goldfarb, DJ Gomer, Sheri Hatch, Mary Hinsley, Laura Horn, Missy Lash, Danielle Lucido, Amy MacDougall, Victoria Oliva, Dianne O'Sullivan, Shannie Pierce, Leigh Miller Poole, Borsie Rich, Elizabeth Rovere, Michele Shannon, Sarah Stuart, Jennifer Wells, and Megan Whyman, you are shiny lights and I am blessed that our paths crossed and we became the Soul Sisters that we are. Thank you for your love, support, and friendship.

Erika Wells, thank you for taking my children on a Disney Cruise with Philippe in January 2012 so I could finish this book. Those silent days of writing were essential to get to the finish line, and you and Philippe made that possible.

Much gratitude to my siblings, Kim, Steve, and John, for your love and support.

And finally, much gratitude to Abraham-Hicks, who first opened my eyes to the Law of Attraction and Deliberate Creation and gave me the nomenclature to teach it to others.

With love, light, and gratitude to you all,

Namaste!

Taylor plus 5

# Contents

*Everything is unfolding as it should.*

# The Beginning

PHOTO: KELLY LORENZ

This book wrote itself, born from my desire to give a big shout out to all of you doing your best to be the best person you can be in each moment. Does this mean being perfect? Absolutely not.

When I created my Super-mom.com blog in May of 2008, I noticed that people sometimes misunderstood my words "Super-mom" and "Super-person" as being a "perfect" Mom or "perfect" person. Not so. I'm here to tell ya, there is no "perfect" and attempting to create or achieve perfection will only bring you suffering.

This book is about the opposite of suffering; it's about empowering you to bring yourself JOY by creating the best life ever, utilizing three Practices. Because you deserve it. Yes, you.

In each chapter you'll see through real-life experiences how I utilize three Practices day-to-day to create the best life ever and learn for yourself how to do the same.

Read this book to tap into, understand, and utilize the three Practices that will help you to create the life of your dreams.

I hope you enjoy reading my words as much as I enjoyed writing them to and for you.

Here's to YOU and creating everything that makes your heart sing, and spreading that JOY and LIGHT to those around you.

Remember, you are a teacher, and what you do matters.

# A Guide To Using This Book

*"It is thought and feeling which guides*
*the Universe, not deeds"*
*- Edgar Cayce*

In this book I will describe to you my formula for creating the best life ever, utilizing three Practices. I will illustrate this formula in action—in real life—with various tales from my life. You will see how you can consistently use my formula to create the best life ever, no matter what is thrown your way. In some chapters I'll spell it out for you, explaining that I used this Practice here and that Practice there. In other chapters it will be clear without my needing to explain.

This formula has worked for me and countless others. I'm all about take what you want and leave the rest, so please do so. If it feels right, go for it. If it doesn't, modify my suggestions or go a completely different route. I'm not saying that this is the right way, the right path, or the only path. I'm saying that it has worked and continues to work for me day in and day out and I'm here to share it with you if you'd like to try something different. I support you and your path, and I'm rootin for ya!

WARNING!

You will feel happy and inspired while and after reading this book and create the best life ever. My intention in writing to you and for you is to uplift, inspire, and support you and help you create your best life ever. I'm writing to and for those who are attracted to this information.

Have the best day ever!

Namaste!

Taylor plus 5

# Chapter 1

# The Best Day Ever: The Three Practices

*My job today is to be in alignment. The rest is up to the Universe and The Law of Attraction.*

"Hi Taylor—I love your blog, and look forward to reading it every 'Mumday'... my word for my day off from work spent with my daughter. I am curious about your path to this bright shiny lightness that you radiate and would love it if you would share some of this. In general I am a happy person but I would love to radiate more light more often. I think I speak for many out there who may not be ready to ask, but how do you honestly and truly have 'the best day ever' every day? I guess I just don't fully understand. I understand that there is a choice in how we react in every situation with which we are faced. Do you have any tips for us on how to make a practice of making the brighter choice every time? And how to make every day—even those when we don't feel great, when our patience isn't at its strongest, etc.—the best day ever? Thanks!"

– A Super-mom.com blog reader

A lot of people ask me how I can honestly have the best day ever every day and I'm happy to share what I personally do to have the best day every day but please remember that my intention for this book and my blogs is for you to find what works for you and brings you joy and follow that no matter what anyone else says. To always follow your heart because then you will always be on the right path. Whatever I say is my humble opinion and what works for me on my path, so please take what you want and leave the rest. I'm never saying, "This is what you should do or that what you're doing is 'wrong,'" because there is no wrong. I'm not perfect nor would I ever profess to be. There's no such thing as "perfect," so please give that up.

What follows is a formula that works for me and has transformed my life in more ways than I can describe. This doesn't mean that this formula will work for you (although it just might and I hope that it does) or that I'm asking you to try it. I'm suggesting that you follow your heart and do what feels right to you, and perhaps this will. I'm putting this out there because many people ask me and this is what works for me. I support all people and the diversity of their choices. There is no right or wrong and there is no perfect. That's what rocks about the Universe.

I've personally found that three Practices are the key to me having the best day ever everyday:

1. Prana Power Yoga

2. Deliberate Creation

3. Foods You Love in Moderation

"But how," you ask, "Do you have time to follow these three Practices daily? With all due respect, life is busy enough and I don't need to add more to my plate."

Oh do I hear you. Loud and clear.

What I have learned is that I don't have time to not do these three things daily. The time and energy that I put in comes back to me, in spades. In spades! Setting my intention and committing to these three Practices shifts my day every day, pointing me in the right direction on my path. They are the key to flowing with life, "trying easy" (as opposed to "trying hard"), finding joy, being super efficient and focused, and having the best day ever every day—no matter what the circumstances. No matter what the circumstances. And oh, just watch how "the circumstances" change.

Let's take it one Practice at a time, and remember you don't have to spend hours on these three Practices every day. Intention and consistency are everything. It's what you do most of the time that matters. There are going to be days that flow well and days that don't. So do what you can and start where you are. It's about being real and doing your best, with breath.

# Practice One: Prana Power Yoga

Do you find it challenging to get to a yoga studio daily or even a few times a week to practice? I hear ya, and I have the solution. Roll out your mat next to your bed before you go to sleep. Wake up a few minutes earlier (yes only minutes) and immediately get on your mat. Immediately! Don't start with your daily routines because then it's all over. I've been there.

Even just doing a rag doll and a downward dog for a few minutes with breath and intention will shift your day and move you toward the best day ever. BUT BEWARE! You may end up practicing longer than you'd planned because it feels so good and just flows.

"But Taylor," you say, "There's so much going on in my life and things come up and life happens. I just can't get to it. I've tried and I just can't."

I get this. I'm all about real life and making things (and these three Practices in particular) accessible. Everyone can do this. Everyone. I've practiced in the pitch black in my bedroom as our two-year-old slept in our bed wheezing with croup and a fever while two humidifiers and the shower filled the room with steam to ease his breathing, poor love. I've practiced on the carpet in our playroom while our two-year-old and five-year-old watched "Elmo" on a projector on the wall (we don't have TV and croup and a fever call for drastic measures) and my two-year-old asked me for water every four minutes or so. These are just two of a myriad of examples of practices that didn't look like the cover of Yoga Journal, although they should—Yoga Journal should get real and put some photos of real life yoga on their covers. My husband and I purposefully put photos on our Prana Power Yoga website of us practicing with our kids running around us. We had a photo shoot once and our kids were with us, as always, and the photographer asked me if he should crop the kids outta the photos and I said, "No way! That's what our practice looks like at home and it's real. Keep 'em in."

So get on your mat, wherever that may be—at home, at a studio, doing my DVD—whatever works and flows. Or if asana ain't yo thang, find something that is that moves energy. You know what you love to do. Maybe it's running or walking or gardening or the elliptical or biking or... reading. A friend of mine swears that reading is "her yoga." And I believe her. She says it moves energy for her like Prana Power Yoga does for me. Rock on!

But what is "yoga" about anyway? People ask me this question a lot. I'll tell you what it's not about. It's not about getting somewhere else. It's about being where you are and being not only OK with where you are, but happy where you are. Happy where you are—imagine that!

So people say to me, "Oh Taylor, that breeds laziness! You're teaching people to be complacent."

Oh no, not so. Yoga teaches us to be happy where we are, and excited for more. Our Spirits will always reach for more because we are always looking for that which will bring us more joy. It's in our nature, our DNA. We can't help but reach for more joy. Think about it, the only reason you want that thing or that accolade or that relationship is because you believe that by having it you will have more joy.

Yoga is about being happy with where you are now as you are in this moment. Not trying to be something or someone else so you can be happy. Somewhat paradoxically, you must be happy to attract whatever you want. You must be at peace with where you are to shift. Until you are, you're stuck. So on your mat you're learning, balancing, breathing—right where you are. And it's all right. Then when you finish your practice you have a sense that everything is all right. You know that you're in the right place at the right time and everything is unfolding as it should. You know that it's a path. You remember who you are.

# Practice Two: Deliberate Creation

"Deliberate Creation" means giving thought to anything is creation and giving deliberate thought to anything is deliberate creation, using the "Law of Attraction." The underlying principle of Deliberate Creation is that our thoughts and our words create our reality. Whatever I give attention to—wanted or unwanted—I am creating. The life I live is created by the story I tell. I enjoy with my action what I created with my thought. I don't create with my action but with my thought.

Our emotions can guide us in this creation process. They can let us know if we're on the path to joy or the alternative. Simply note your emotions and when you feel negative emotion, that's your emotional guidance system doing its job to guide you. It's letting you know that your thoughts aren't on track to creating your best life ever.

Taking all of these principles into account, I have learned to relax and let the Law of Attraction do the organization and the managing while I spend my time doing the things I love. I utilize my thoughts, words, and feelings to "manifest" (another word for intentionally create) whatever I want, creating the best life ever.

Does this mean that I lie around all day doing nothing? Not at all. I believe in and love massive action. But I do things that I love so it don't feel like "work" and it all flows beautifully and easily.

Sound too good to be true? It's not. It's taken time and practice to get to this place of loving everything that I do and everyone in my life and (just about) all of the situations I draw into my life, but the practice is fun and continues day to day. The practice is my life. My best life ever.

In any situation I have a choice, a choice on what to focus my mind. It's all about the power of the focus of my mind. In any situation you can focus on the stuff that's great or the stuff that's not. Some call this denial. I call it focusing on what I want to see and thereby creating the future I want utilizing The Law of Attraction.

I spent a few years of my life doing otherwise—feeling angry, afraid, resentful, and talking and writing about it a lot. What I learned during those times was that whatever I put out came back to me multiplied. This was not a good thing at the time, taking into account what I was putting out to the Universe.

There are absolutely times when we need to grieve and mourn and the only way out is through. But there are also many times when we have a choice on what to focus. We have a choice what to talk about. We have a choice what to think about.

A few years ago I took our then eleven-year-old daughter Madison to a café in our neighborhood for a surprise breakfast before school. The tables were bunched close together and we couldn't help but hear the women's conversation at the table next to us. They were going on and on about negative stuff—some call it gossip. The energy emanating from that table was pretty dark. Even my eleven-year-old daughter felt it. What were those two women creating by saying this about that friend and that about this child? What kind of day were they setting up for themselves? How would their hearts feel after they finished that mochachino?

It took me a while to learn not to gossip. And even longer for my friends to get used to me not joining in. I still occasionally get drawn into the practice of gossip but feel the results immediately after doing so, yet another reminder to stay on my path. Remember, no one is perfect (including me) and it's what we do most of the time that matters. We all stumble or fall at times. With practice we learn to be gentle with ourselves, get up, and try again. The Universe will always give us "contrast" to show us what it is that we don't want in our lives so we can create what we do want. Every person walking this planet experiences contrast. It's important to remember this while creating the best life ever utilizing the three Practices. Our Spirits want and need contrast to grow and evolve—to know what we do want. This said, we can train ourselves to grow and evolve through joy, love, and ease. We can make our moments of contrast brief and mostly painless. By utilizing the three Practices we can finesse our experiences day-to-day into our best life ever by being awake, aware, and open to what the Universe lays out in front of us.

## We have a choice on what to focus.

But how do you stay on the path of positive thinking and manifesting in a world that can be super negative? What about when something really sucks?

> "I love the positive stories on your blog, but I get even more when you share your moments of contrast. Knowing that even bright shiny people like you and Philippe sometimes experience difficult things reminds me that things don't have to be 'best ever' all the time, and that when they're not, the best thing to do is admit it, let go, and move on. Light and love to you all."
>
> – A Best Life Ever blog reader

People sometimes tell me that it's easy to accept and take responsibility for our lives when they're going well but what about when they're not? I get it. I get that when things go "bad" it: A. Don't feel good, and B. Don't feel possible to take responsibility for it.

I had a rough childhood so it ain't always been incense and cupcakes for this Super-mom. I believe that my Spirit chose my parents to create the contrast to show me quite clearly and quite early what I do want. My childhood taught me to find the light in any situation and focus on it. My childhood taught me to be the Spiritual being I was born to be. My childhood taught me to be a leader, a survivor, and a thriver instead of a victim.

I was brought up to "succeed." To get straight A's and be "the best" at whatever I was doing—that that was my "purpose." In retrospect it was healthy for me at the time because it distracted me from the painful stuff going on in my childhood home.

Now many years later I've learned that my purpose is to be happy. Paradoxically, from that happy place, expansion is inevitable. So it's not, "If I do this or if I have that, I will be happy," but instead, "I'm happy now and therefore everything I want to be, do, and have flows effortlessly to me." The energy of my joy brings it to me, like a magnet. This is law. The Law of Attraction.

Most people have it backwards, as I did for decades, saying and thinking, "I gotta work hard, life is hard, it's supposed to be hard, no one is really happy—but when I have this or am that, then I'll be happy."

Start now finding gratitude and joy in this moment for something. Anything. Let that energy pervade your entire being. Feel it in your heart. Practice this until joy is your vibration most of the time, unless you're experiencing contrast, which is simply showing you what you want to ask for. Then ask for that—what you do want, let go of all thoughts of the contrast, and find joy and gratitude again. Remember, your purpose is to be happy. From there, expansion and everything you've been asking for is inevitable. Find the happiness first.

What I have personally learned again and again through pain, sorrow, and heartbreak is that if I can take responsibility and ask the Universe what the lesson is, what I need to learn, what I need to do differently, then the clarity comes and I move higher. Higher vibration. More joy. More love. More clarity. More flow. More magic.

Is it a life without heartbreak? Sorrow? Grief? Absolutely not. Those things are a part of life, even the best life ever, because they provide us with the contrast, which shows us what it is we don't want to further clarify what it is that we do want. But this is where most people slip up and this is why I'm explaining the concept of contrast a few times and why I will continue to remind you about it throughout this book. It takes a while to really take in the concept so most people repeatedly beat the drum of what went wrong, what they didn't like, what stinks, etc. and thereby draw more of that to themselves via the Law of Attraction.

The intention day in and day out is to focus our minds on that which we do want and not the opposite. As we do so, as we become the masters of our minds (it's all about the power of the focus of your mind), the contrast becomes infrequent and brief. We live a lot more of what we do want. We live the best life ever.

But don't try to control your negative thoughts. Just like worrying is using your imagination to create something you don't want, trying to control your negative thoughts just brings more of "needing to control your thoughts" into your life. Like a magnet.

Instead, simply begin to train your mind to focus on that which you do want instead of what you don't want. It's a skill—a practice—just like yoga, the first Practice. The more you practice the more you'll be able to utilize the power of the focus of your mind so you're not trying to control negative thoughts but turning your attention and your thoughts to what you do want. Again and again. One moment at a time.

It's all about choices. I chose to give up watching TV fourteen years ago and never looked back. I watch DVD's occasionally but am deliberate about choosing those with good energy. Not watching TV really helped me to decrease the amount of negative messages infiltrating my brain, many unconsciously.

I choose to write down quotes that I love—uplifting, positive quotes that I read, hear, or come up with myself—and read them as often as possible. They are all over my house. At my computer, on my kitchen counter tops, next to my toothbrush, on my desk, and in front of my yoga mat. I write them on my iPhone and read them every morning when I do cardio at the Y. Whenever and wherever possible I am putting positive messages into my brain. I am always watching my mind and training it. Much like I trained myself to hit a tennis ball thirty-three years ago at Nick Bollettieri's Tennis Academy, it just takes practice.

Marianne Williamson said that she asks the Universe, "Where would you have me go? What would you have me do? What would you have me say and to whom?" Inspired by her words I created this mantra which I use daily while utilizing the second Practice, "Universe please light the path for me. Please give me wisdom, clarity, and guidance regarding what to do and when, what to say and to whom, and what to eat and drink so that I am a happy Super-mom to my five children, healthy, strong, a clear channel for your love and  light, in the Vortex all day and night, totally calm, clear, focused, at peace, effective, efficient, productive, inspired, and of service." Feel free to use this mantra if it speaks to you or make up one of your own.

## Practice Three: Foods You Love in Moderation*

Do you find it scary and unappealing to restrict what you eat? Do you feel restricted even reading the word "restriction?" I hear ya. Creating the best life ever is definitely not about restriction. Restriction and deprivation don't work, and they're no fun. If you're going to have the best day ever every day, it's all about fun. Most likely, no one taught you this growing up and in fact, they may have taught you that you have to work hard and sacrifice to be successful. But I'm here to tell ya that you become even more efficient, effective, productive, and "successful" when you're having fun. How 'bout that?

Please re-read the last two sentences and really take them in. You're undoing years of programming that is both wrong and unhelpful so it's gonna take discipline and practice for you to reprogram yourself.

Eating the foods you love in moderation is all about intention and doing your best with breath, as is Prana Power Yoga and Deliberate Creation. It's all connected, which makes it easier and more fun. It all flows together, beautifully and easily. You simply set your intention, "I want to have the best day ever every day," and start where you are to begin to allow yourself to eat the foods you love in moderation whenever you want.

"Wait!" you may be saying, "I have issues with over-eating Taylor, and I absolutely cannot eat cupcakes or pasta or potato chips. Or carbs of any kind, for that matter. Once I start, I can't stop!"

Oh I hear ya and I get it. Here's the difference though. This time you're doing it differently because you're incorporating the other two Practices of creating the best life ever concurrently. You're practicing Prana Power Yoga or your equivalent "yoga" and Deliberate Creation regularly and in doing so balancing and grounding yourself so you will naturally gravitate to and love the foods that your body, mind, and Spirit are craving and need. And even if in the moment that food is doughnuts for whatever reason (and every reason is OK, there's no judgment or "good" or "bad" foods. Remember, it's all about the power of the focus of your mind), you will eat as many of those doughnuts as feels good physically, emotionally, and Spiritually, and then move on. Without the aftermath of regret, guilt, stagnant energy, and weight gain. No aftermath! And in doing so, you will be empowered in such a way that makes the first two Practices even easier. Every Practice builds on the other and when they're all utilized regularly with discipline, your life becomes pure magic. Magic!

I utilize the three Practices all day every day, and I gotta say, it's way more fun to practice having the best day ever than to practice hitting backhands.

*In the first draft of this book that was set to go to print in the spring of 2011, the third Practice of creating the best life ever was "raw vegan foods." My family and I had been raw vegan for seven years and I believed that eating high vibration food was key—along with Prana Power Yoga and Deliberate Creation—to creating the life of your dreams. In a synchronistic turn of events, my manuscript was lost in an airport that spring, delaying the publication of this book. Not coincidentally, a few months later my husband and I chose to stop being a label and in doing so were blessed with wisdom about true freedom. I then rewrote this book with this new wisdom. Good thing I lost my manuscript in that airport!

# Chapter 2

# Choosing the Best Thought Ever

Giving thought to anything is creation.
Giving deliberate thought to anything
is Deliberate Creation.

As I opened the Word file of this chapter to proof it I realized that I had inadvertently lost the chapter in a "Microsoft Word saving mishap."

Bummer!

I felt "that" feeling—that negative feeling that usually accompanies an experience where you lose something you wrote, bought, had, loved, etc. And that ain't a fabulous feeling. Then come the thoughts. Whatever thoughts you conjure up when you have a less-than-optimal experience. Everyone's thoughts have different flavors, different intensities. But with time, armed with the knowledge of The Law of Attraction and the desire to deliberately create your life—the best life ever! —you can and will learn how to redirect your thoughts immediately and indeed choose the best thought ever in any situation.

Let's take the example of losing the copy of this chapter. Upon realizing I'd lost the chapter I had "a moment." Then I let it go and immediately focused on another chapter. This was my (quite effective) distraction from the negative thoughts, utilizing Deliberate Creation.

It's easy, so listen up.

Later I came back to this chapter to make sure that it had indeed been lost. Yes, it had. "OK, so that's done," I thought to myself, "and it must be for some higher good. The Universe only closes a door when it's going to open another—even better—one." I continued. "I'm going to write another—even better—chapter right now."

Then the negative thoughts stopped because I was back in "The Vortex," where all love, joy, dreams, inspiration, magic, and creativity are experienced. When I write I abide in the Vortex. Pretty much anyone who writes easily and joyfully does. Time stands still and I feel nothing but love, joy, focus, inspiration, and good energy flowing through me. It's magical.

So there I was, back in the Vortex, enjoying everything I was typing to and for you—yeah, you, because I wrote this book for you. Those other thoughts and that experience were a distant memory. I had utilized Deliberate Creation effectively.

As I explained in chapter 1, we all have examples of contrast in our lives—situations or experiences that we would rather not be living—so that our Spirits know what we do want to be living and can immediately begin to create that which we want. What holds us—and our Spirits—back from the creation process is only one thing: "resistance." Resistance comes in three forms: thoughts, feelings, and actions. Sometimes—often times if we are not "deliberate creators"—we are not even aware of our resistance. And this is where and why things ain't a-happenin' for us. This is why we say things like, "The best life ever? Gimme a break. I'm barely gettin' by, Sister."

I hear you. Oh do I hear you. Been there, done that.

But here's the key—the shift—and it's easy, so listen up. All that's necessary is that you are aware. Once you are aware of your thoughts and your emotions, you can guide them and therefore your actions, toward the best life ever. All it takes is practice. So practice, practice, practice Deliberate Creation.

"But how," you ask, "Can I do that? How can I be aware and how do I practice?" Well, you're already on the right track, so smile. You were magnetized to this book and are now reading it with an open mind and an open heart, so you're halfway there. Now just notice. Notice when you have a negative emotion. Notice when you have a negative thought.

At first this may be quite disconcerting because you may have them all the time. That's OK. No worries. Just breathe and notice. All of your power is in this moment—in the NOW—and you can be, do, and have anything that you want. Just begin to do your best to shift the thoughts.

Tools to shift the thoughts? The three Practices to create the best life ever.

## Practice one:
### Move negative energy out of your body every single day.

I personally find Prana Power Yoga very effective in doing this, but if yoga ain't yo' thang, find something that is that moves energy for you.

What does "move energy" mean? Everything is energy. As we walk this planet day-to-day, energy gets accumulated in our mental and physical bodies. It's necessary to clean and clear this energy out regularly, much like it's necessary to take out the trash in your kitchen regularly. Yoga and the breathing that accompanies it are the best way I've found to do this. If you aren't into yoga you might take a run or a walk in nature or swim or garden or meditate or whatever works for you. This is a personal choice and it's all good.

## Practice two:
### Think thoughts that feel good.

"How do I do this?" you ask. "I tend to be so negative in my thinking because I have this thing, that thing, and this other thing in my life that really stink. And they're all true. It's my reality, Taylor."

I hear you, but remember that "truth" is only a thought you've had over and over. "Truth" is only a thought you keep thinking. And "reality" is just your practiced truth. You have the POWER to change that thought and therefore your truth RIGHT NOW. It just takes practice. As you do it—even for a moment—you'll begin to feel the relief. And as you feel the relief, you're on the path.

Just find the best-feeling thought you can, and focus on it. It's not your "job" to focus on the other stuff, regardless if it's "true" or "reality" or not. Focus, focus, focus on what feels good, and watch your life turn around. Witness your life and your world transform. One thought at a time. You can do this, and the results will be instantaneous and nothing less than miraculous. So begin now. This is the perfect time.

Now what was that thought you just had?

# Practice three:
## Eat the foods you love in moderation.

Empower yourself to live a life of freedom in every aspect of your life, including the foods you consume. Stop the restriction. Stop the deprivation. Begin allowing in all areas of your life instead of resisting. If you are allowing the natural flow of the Universe in your life you can create anything that you want; however, if you are doing so in all areas of your life but you are still restricting in one area—what you eat or whatever—and thereby limiting your freedom, there's only so much good you are allowing into your life. You can get all emotional about this and argue with me that this isn't true and tell me all the reasons why you can't eat whatever you want and why you have to restrict what types of food you eat, but that ain't gonna help you create the best life ever. The Law of Attraction is real. If you're tired of the whole dieting game (and how's it goin' for ya so far? Let's face facts. Diets don't work, and you and I both know it) then listen up and get ready to live real change and find and feel freedom—real freedom in all areas of your life.

The more you practice Prana Power Yoga and Deliberate Creation, the easier this third Practice will become. The more you will be able to actually eat anything and everything you want and as much as you want whenever you want and feel great and be the healthiest and happiest weight for you. Anyone can eat anything that they want in moderation provided that when they eat they are in check with their thoughts and beliefs about eating and their weight.

It's my experience after being 100% raw vegan for seven years that I feel and look better now eating all foods in moderation than I did when I'd eat ginormous salads and raw vegan meals that were over the top quantity and nutrient wise—arguably the most nutritious food I could eat—but left me digesting for way too many hours. The digesting process took it outta me and "weighed me down" (pun-intended), even though the food was supreme and in its purest form. Digesting those huge raw vegan meals taxed my organs and sapped my energy. Adhering to a label and therefore restricting my freedom (and thereby resisting) also sapped my energy. Ironically, it was all a big energy drain. Ironic because the raw vegan lifestyle is supposed to give you energy, not drain it. After dropping the raw vegan label of seven years it's now my personal understanding that any form of restriction and deprivation that keeps you from your ultimate freedom will decrease your energy and life force. Even and especially if it's unconscious.

For example, I feel better now physically and energetically if I eat a moderate amount of "True Whip" (my favorite non dairy whipped topping) than if I eat a big serving of a raw vegan nut loaf. I believe that it's the quantity that you eat at one time that matters more so than what specific food you're eating at any given time. And so even if you're eating perfectly crafted amazing high vibration food, if you overeat it (as many people do because deep down they're feeling deprived on some level), you'd be better off having a moderate amount of brown rice and steamed veggies (or a few spoonfuls of cookie dough or whatever you're craving) and calling it a day. In addition, clinical studies show that eating until three quarters full positively affects longevity. Many centenarians report that they've eaten moderately over their life span, eating all types of food in moderation. Remember it's not about being perfect because there ain't no such thang. Even the centenarians chowed down (overate) once in a while. It's what you do most of the time that matters.

I also believe in mixing up what you eat. So not ever getting into a routine where you eat the exact same things day in and day out. Always keeping your body guessing is a sure way, in my humble opinion, to keep it happy, healthy, and lean. Think of it as the cross training of eating, if you will.

Remember, it's about being real and doing your best, with breath. You'll find that if you let go of the fear (utilizing Prana Power Yoga and Deliberate Creation), you'll naturally gravitate to the foods which your body, mind, and Spirit love, and a balanced amount of them at any given time for you to feel happy, satisfied, grounded, and free.

# Chapter 3

# What's Your Intention?

*"Our intention creates our reality."*
*- Wayne Dyer*

PHOTO: RAY MUCCI

A helpful tool when cultivating and utilizing Deliberate Creation while creating the best life ever is setting an intention during the transitions of your day. For example, before you get out of bed in the morning, take a minute to set an intention for your day. It don't have to be fancy or long—just the gist. Something like," I wanna be happy" will work great.

As you're moving into your morning routine of brushing your teeth, getting dressed, eating your breakfast, etc., set an intention for that.

As you get on your yoga mat, set an intention for your practice. As you drive to work, school, errands, or wherever your path takes you, set an intention for that segment of your day. Remember it doesn't have to be complicated or long. It can even be just one word, like "peace" or "love" or "clarity" or "joy" or "ease."

Start now. Before you step into the next portion of your day today take a moment to set an intention. Then watch what happens.

What's your intention for reading this book?

# Chapter 4

# Super-mom

"The words 'I am...' are potent words; be careful
what you hitch them to. The thing you're claiming
has a way of reaching back and claiming you."
- A.L. Kitselman

"I'm so overwhelmed." "I have too much on my plate." "I have three kids and no time for me." "I have no time for yoga." "How DO you do it all?"

I hear this all the time. As a Mom, how do we give our all to our children and maintain our joy for life?

Two words: Super Mom.

I have five kids—ages fourteen, eight, five, two, and two (twin boys), five yoga studios, five blogs, practice and teach yoga and do cardio every day, am always energized, and have the best day ever, every day.

"How is this possible?" You ask, wondering how a person so full of herself could be a yogi.

This is not arrogance, it's energetic. It's not about ego; it's about "vibration." The words you use, the thoughts you think, the feelings you have, and the actions you take determine your vibration.

Vibration is a way to calibrate how it feels to be around someone. Think of someone you love to be around... what is it about her? Is it what she wears? (No.) Is it what she drives? (No.) Is it where she lives? (No.) It's her vibration. She has good energy. Do you?

It's an attitude. A choice. You are the artist of your life—painting with your thoughts, emotions, words, and actions. What are you painting?

In a busy world with constant stimulation and deadlines, it's easy to slip into victim mode if we aren't mindful.

We've all had "that" moment—probably more times than we care to recall: you're late to your three-year-old's teacher conference, the baby poops as you're walking out the door, the phone is ringing with an issue that needs to be dealt with immediately, and the school nurse is calling on your cell phone to say that your seven-year-old daughter fell, ripped her pants, and wants a new pair and some Mommy love—now.

Here's where the choice comes in (Deliberate Creation). You can go into victim mode and fall apart, coming from drama and the land of the overwhelmed, or you can come from empowerment and declare, "I am Super-Mom!" breathe through the moment, and then proceed, dealing with one thing at a time with grace, finding joy in each moment—your baby's smile as you change his diaper, the sparkle in your three-year-old's teacher's eyes as she tells you how wonderful your child is, the gratitude on your seven-year-old daughter's face as you walk into her classroom with a fresh pair of jeans.

This is it. This is the only moment that matters. Finding joy in this moment is how we become the joyful person we want to be, and, ironically, more time will be available to us. Because the more you choose to be Super-Mom, the more you will be Super-Mom.

Your kids, partner, friends, and colleagues are counting on you. But mostly, you are counting on you. You're the one making the choice to have that thought. Choose wisely, Super-Mom.

# Chapter 5

# Does The Law of Attraction Discriminate?

*"You are a living magnet; you attract into your life people, situations, and circumstances that are in harmony with your dominant thoughts. Whatever you dwell on in the conscious grows in your experience."*
*- Brian Tracy*

"I'm happy that you're living the best life ever and are so beautiful and successful just 'going with the flow' of the Universe. But what about others who pursue their heart and just get knocked down again and again. What about those who are physically unattractive and ignored by the opposite sex? Did they create their own loneliness? Something about your 'Universe co-creating' thing seems like it just won't work for everyone. If you're walking down the street and you get robbed or mugged did you co-create it? It's reassuring to think the Universe will 'take care of you,' but it sure hasn't done that for me...."
— A Best Life Ever blog reader

It takes time, focus, intention, and discipline to teach yourself how to say thank you when someone is unkind to you. To say thank you when you fall on yo a** in whatever you're doin'. To say thank you when you get rejected, yet again. It all comes down to the power of the focus of your mind, and if you can train yourself to say thank you in the midst of challenge, to stay calm and focused in a challenging moment, you got it made and will create the best life ever.

Begin to accept now that you drew those experiences to yourself via the Law of Attraction. Your Spirit chose that situation, that experience, and that event to bring you to a new place. To provide contrast so that by seeing what you don't want, you will know more clearly what you do want. So you be movin to a new place thanks to that situation. Unless you're resisting. Resisting often takes the form of focusing on the "bad" thing that happened and why you want it to be different and beating the drum of that again and again, instead of acknowledging the contrast and then utilizing Deliberate Creation to focus on (talk, write, think about) what it is that you do want.

After teaching yourself to say thank you for whatever comes your way—to find gratitude for the contrast—the challenge becomes to allow. Allow yourself to focus on what you do want instead of what you don't want (which you just experienced). You can start with a simple mantra like, "I choose to allow only good things in my life" or "I choose to focus on that which I do want." Or "thank you mind, for that information (the focus on the unwanted thing) but I only focus on what I want." You wouldn't say, "I choose to allow, not resist good things" or "I choose to not focus on the bad things that have happened" because the Universe don't hear or acknowledge negatives (not) and so you'll be drawing in more resistance with those words.

Law of Attraction ain't picky. It don't discriminate. It don't judge. It simply returns to you precisely what you put out. There are no exceptions. This is law. So yes, you get what you put out there. Period.

I know full well I be openin' myself up to get slammed with that statement ("Yeah, easy for you to say, you've always had it easy, you're this and you're that and that makes it all so easy for you. You have no idea what I been through Sister.") but I'm here to tell ya that I've been to hell and back. I'm living and breathing proof that the Law of Attraction works because you don't even wanna hear about where I came from. Yet through the darkness—the pitch black—I held on to my faith that I would "get out" of that life of darkness and create a life of joy. I knew I was different than those around me who were shrouded in darkness. I knew I was light, as are you. I chose to focus on something— anything—that I could find that was positive in the dark situations that permeated my early years on this planet.

## You get what you put out there.

After surviving everything I did I was hell bent on writin' a book about it. Until I learned about Deliberate Creation (which I'd been practicing since birth, unbeknownst to me). After learning about the Law of Attraction, I made a different choice. I chose to leave the rat race, open a yoga studio, and spread the light.

Now that light comes back to me multiplied on a daily basis. Multiplied.

The thing about Law of Attraction is that it's fun and easy to take responsibility for the good stuff, but when something sucks, well, we can't believe that we created it. We wanna say we caused the good, but the bad? We don't even wanna look at it let alone take responsibility for it. And while this is human (hey, I been there), it's problematic.

I've seen how the law works again and again and I therefore take responsibility for every single thing that comes onto my path and when it's not the best ever, I stop and ask myself how and why I created it and what the lesson is. I ask what I need to learn and what I need to do differently. I ask what thoughts, actions, words, and emotions drew the experience to me. I ask, wait for clarity, listen, learn, and begin again. It's a path.

Can you see the POWER in this? Can you see the power you have?

# Chapter 6

# But Why Is Negative Thinking Easier to Fall Into Than Positive Thinking?

PHOTO: MEGAN GEORGE

Everything around you is an extension
of a previous thought and vibration.

"Negative thinking seems to be an easier rut to fall into than positive--why is that? We all want to believe the best about others, why are we so quick to be harsh or negative with ourselves?"
– A Best Life Ever blog reader

This question pertains specifically to Deliberate Creation and is an important thing to understand as you embark on this journey of creating the best life ever.

If negative thinking seems to be easier for you than positive, that's what your habit of thinking is. It's that simple. Remember, the Law of Attraction doesn't discriminate. It just sends back to you what you're putting out, akin to the law of gravity. Gravity doesn't choose, "OK, this one I'm gonna apply the law to but not that one." If you pick up a shoe and let go of it, that shoe gonna drop. Similarly, if you thinkin' negative thoughts, more negative thoughts are comin' yo' way.

We are not "so quick to be harsh and negative with ourselves" at birth. We learn this pattern and practice it again and again.

The great news is that with awareness (which you now have, congratulations!), you can change this pattern, in an instant. Simply utilize the three Practices I'm describing and you're on the path. It works.

# Chapter 7

# The "Re-vision": What To Do When Something Goes "Wrong"

*"Imagination is everything. It is the preview of life's coming attractions."*
*- Albert Einstein*

What do you do when something goes "wrong" or not the way you wanted it to go? The usual response is to ruminate and metaphorically kick yourself in the a** repeatedly for it. Stop doing this.

"But what then should I do?" you ask. "I feel so bad about what happened and how I behaved and I can't get it outta my mind, Taylor."

OK, no worries. Remain calm, and eat a cupcake.

Kidding! Just wanted to lighten the mood a bit.

And that's the point, lighten the mood. Lighten the mood, lighten your mind. Lighten the mood, lighten your body. Lighten the mood, lighten your life. It's all about the light.

Here's what I recommend. As you get into bed that night—and every night—review the day's events. If any events or moments didn't go the way you wanted, replay them in your mind in a way that thrills you. I call this "re-visioning". As you recreate the events in your mind exactly as you want ("re-vision"), you're cleaning up your frequency from the day and emitting a new frequency for tomorrow. You're rewiring your memory and more importantly, your energy. You're intentionally creating new pictures for your future. The Universe don't know if your energy is from what you're experiencing or imagining. Lemme say that again because it's key. The Universe don't know if your energy is from what you're experiencing or imagining. It will match that energy immediately, sending you people, places, and things that match that energy. This is the Law of Attraction at work. "Re-visioning" your day is Deliberate Creation in action.

So if you be ruminating, you be creating more of what happened that you didn't like or want. You are saying to the Universe, "Please send me more of this." I know you don't want more of it but the Universe don't discriminate or judge or choose, remember? It just sends back to you exactly what you're putting out. It is law.

Here's one example of oh-so-many I could tell you. Philippe, Sagey (age seven at the time), Phoenix (age five at the time), Dakota (age one at the time) and Montana (age one at the time) were flying in at 3 pm after a week away on a Disney cruise with Philippe's mom. Super-mom and Madison (age fourteen at the time) didn't join because Madison didn't wanna miss school and I wanted to finish this book. I'd written it in seven weeks almost two years prior and as Philippe joked, "Let's just get it out there." I'd had the twins, lost a hard copy of the final manuscript in an airport, stopped being a label, sold the restaurant, and stopped homeschooling, and girlfriend's book needed a rewrite big-time; but the day-to-day of raising five kids, running five yoga studios, and writing five blogs had meant it wasn't a-happenin'.

We talked to a few friends who've published books and they said that yes they had to go away to finish their books—to "get away from the everyday." On a walk one day Philippe said, "You gotta go away to finish the book, Super-mom." I glanced at my twins smiling up at me from the baby-jogger and said, "Ugh I don't wanna pump and leave everybody for a week, and how would you handle it? All five without me?"

The Universe stepped in and synchronized events as only it can. Philippe and his mom took four of our five kids on the cruise; the twins had weaned themselves naturally by then; and everyone won. Philippe loves Disney and cruises and I don't, and I finished my book with all of the hours of quiet focus and clear intention.

So what was the uh, not best ever experience then? The re-entry. Here's how it went down.

Philippe asked me to be at the airport at 3:45 pm and I was lined up to do so. I'd write till three, pick up Madison from her friend's house at 3:15, and we'd have plenty of time to get to the airport. No one likes to be kept waiting at the airport, with four young kids no less.

As I was leaving I got an urgent text about something at Prana Power Yoga, paused to respond to it, and then got a text from Philippe saying they'd gotten in early. Oops! I scooted out the door to pickup Madison, concerned that they'd be waiting for us at the airport. When I arrived at her friend's house she wasn't ready. I waited several minutes as my anxiety grew and my energy tanked. Once Madison got in the car I was seething. We were now officially late and I was triggered by all the times my ex-husband had been late in our eighteen years together. My button had been pushed and even with all I know about the Law of Attraction and energy (I knew better!) Super-mom hit the roof. Madison and I bickered as we sped to the airport, arriving ironically at exactly 3:45 pm, the time Philippe had originally requested. But I'm a strong manifester and so even though Madison and I had made up and said we were sorry before we arrived at the airport, the energetic wheels were in motion. Plus, as I realized later that evening, I'd forgotten to envision how I wanted the day and the re-entry to flow, so the Universe was just giving me what I had put out energetically. As it always does. No exceptions.

I highly recommend using your imagination to see and feel how you want things to go (which I hadn't done regarding the re-entry). It works, and is the essence of Deliberate Creation. I'd been so focused on finishing the book in those last hours of quiet, I'd totally forgotten.

It started in the car driving home from the airport. Montana was crying and all the kids were talking at once as Philippe was trying to tell me about the whole trip in a twelve-minute car ride. I smiled, found gratitude that my precious family was home safe and sound, and surrendered to the chaos of a family of seven.

We arrived home and I excitedly showed Philippe his "new office" that I'd had re-painted while they were away. "Ohhhhh, it's, uh, 'nice,'" he lied. "You don't like it?" I cried. "I liked it better before," he admitted.

Montana was still crying, Phoenix was whining for his gummy vitamins, Dakota wouldn't let me put him down, Sagey and Madison were talking a mile a minute to me—at the same time—vying for Super-mom's attention, and Philippe was pissed because the painter had messed up his Mac cord so his computer wouldn't turn on.

I paused for a moment and remembered a "Calgon take me away" ad from the 70's with a smile.

I made dinner amidst the half unpacked suitcases and toys and clothes and other clutter strewn about (what happens in an instant when five kids descend upon any dwelling), and breathed in and breathed out mindfully, attempting to listen as best as I could to the myriad of stories being tossed in my direction concurrently.

My kids had missed me and they all wanted a piece of Super-mom, who was feeling oddly unable to balance it all and give each child what they needed. This coupled with the fact that Philippe didn't like my "big surprise" didn't feel the best ever, and my energy continued to tank, mostly because I'm extremely sensitive to energy so when it goin' downhill it goes downhill fast, as will yours as you become more attune to energy. The Universe will let you know loud and clear that you off-kilter, so you can clean up your energy fast.

Before I went I sleep that night I went to Madison's room and chatted with her and Sagey about what had gone down and said I was sorry it hadn't flowed more smoothly. "Huh?" they both asked, clueless about what I was talking about. They'd experienced it all very differently. Then Madison said, "Mom, ya gotta let it go. We love you and everyone missed you and you did the best you could. Be gentle with yourself."

I smiled, thanked her for her wisdom, and tucked myself into my bed, re-visioning how it all went down in a way that made me happy. And I gotta say, it was gooood in my revisionist history. Now that's a revisionist history I stand behind. It was beautiful and flowing and calm and happy, complete with us all eating at the dining room table with candles and incense lit, enjoying the welcome home chocolate cake I'd put out next to a sparkly welcome home sign. (In take one no one had noticed the cake let alone consumed it).

You don't have to act on imagination. Just imagine and have good energy. That's enough. The Universe will take care of the rest. Leave the details and the organization up to the Universe and just imagine and have fun. Manifestation comes from consistent vibration and consistent visualization. Be committed to the feeling of your imagination.

# Chapter 8

# Why I Stopped Being A Label

*"Don't worry that children never listen to you;*
*worry that they are always watching you."*
*- Robert Fulghum*

It started with my children.

I operate from my heart most of the time, but where my children are concerned, it's 100% of the time. This was no different. And when you are really operating straight from your heart and Spirit, there is clarity and speed.

We were taking a ferry to Nantucket with our plus five. My husband Philippe and I were very sick, had fevers, and hadn't slept or eaten much in days. We *never* get sick.

On the ferry a Super-mom came up to me and said, "Oh my God! I love your blogs and Prana Power Yoga! And I have twins too! And they're Dakota and Montana's age!"

And there they were. Her twins. Except I was confused... they were about as tall as Philippe.

I never compare my kids to other people's kids. This Super-mom has learned that only leads to suffering. But this—this caught my attention.

Enter Super-mom number two a few minutes later. She essentially said the exact same thing, showed me her (ginormous) twins, and my stomach dropped.

Then, I kid you not, a third Super-mom approached me on that (one hour!) ferry ride, said she loved my blogs and Prana, and had... twins my twins' age. At this point I looked around for a camera. "Do they still film candid camera?" I wondered. There were no cameras. This wasn't a joke. In a one-hour period three women had approached me with twins my twins' age, yet their twins were all much bigger than mine. My heart sank and my stomach ached. I fought back tears as I told myself what I believe, "All kids grow at their own rate and in their own time. Don't compare. That's ridiculous."

My mind fought back, "I've never once even thought about my (other three older) kids being 'little.' They were always big and healthy, a size bigger than their 'actual age' in clothes. Hmmmm, but wait, not Phoenix, come to think of it (my four-year-old who had been raw vegan since birth.) Only my girls who ate everything with no restriction were like that."

I told myself that it was OK, that I was sick and weak and emotional. Tomorrow I'd feel better and be clearer. I would wait for the muddy waters to settle (The Tao).

The next day, I wouldn't have believed it if I weren't there myself... the Universe sent me another Super-mom with twins my twins' age. Same story. Same drop in my stomach. Except this time we were at a beach club celebrating my niece's birthday and my father in law pointed out loudly, "Wow! They're only a week apart?"

He didn't say the obvious, that her twins were huge and half again as big as mine, but it was hangin' there like a silent bubble on a cartoon.

I made it to the car before bursting into tears and turned to my husband and said, "Our kids are no longer raw vegan."

"Whuuuut?!" gasped Philippe.

"Did you see those twins?" I asked incredulously. "That's the 4th time that that's happened to me in twenty-four hours! The Universe is speaking, loud and clear. And I'm listening!"

Philippe started to go into a diatribe about how in this country kids eat a lot of hormones and so they're bigger, but I jumped right in and said, "We live in this country!" And our boys live with kids in this country and at this rate, they're gonna be five feet tall at age seventeen and say, 'Hey, thanks, Mom!' Philippe, you're six feet tall and I'm five foot seven. They should be bigger."

My husband paused, and then said something he don't say often, "I'm sorry. You're right."

"There's no longitudinal research about raw vegan kids!" I continued, "And we don't know any 100% raw vegan kids. What does that say?"

Philippe and I had lived two years as raw vegans before including our kids in our raw vegan lifestyle. We had wanted to make sure it was all it was cracked up to be. But in the now, in that moment, the answer, and the path, was clear.

We got back to the little beach house we'd rented and put the twins down for a nap, chatting all the while excitedly. "What are we gonna feed them?" I asked. Remember, it had been seven years since we'd eaten anything besides raw vegan food. "Lots of dairy and meat with lots of hormones, " Philippe quipped. "That's why all the kids in this country are so big." He was kidding, sort of. "Well, we don't have to do THAT," I said. "I was thinking... Cheerios?"

Were we really doing this?

Then I asked Philippe if it was OK for me to tell his family. They were all waiting back at the beach club for me to return for lunch and a part of me felt like I was dreaming. Were we really doing this? Was it really happening? I also come from a trauma history and as a child there were lots of secrets in my family of origin, so I'm sure that had something to do with it. "Sure!" Philippe said cheerfully, and off I went to the club to tell his family the big news.

I ran up to Philippe's mom, sister, and Madison, our (then) thirteen-year-old daughter, all sitting poolside and burst into tears (again). "What is it?" they all asked. I told them the whole story between sniffles and quiet sobs. Madison hugged me and said, "Mom, I'm so proud of you. You committed to something that you really believed in even though no one else was doing it. You followed your heart. It was way harder to be raw vegan for the last seven years than to eat a standard American diet. Now you've had a strong intuition and you are immediately changing your plan. You aren't saying, 'Oh, I'm right, this is right,' and trying to prove you've been right. You are just cleaning the slate and beginning again right now."

I stared at Madison, wise beyond her years, said thank you, and then told her that of course I would change any plan once I had any inkling that it wasn't going well. The moment I had such an inkling. It wasn't about ego; it was about the health and happiness of my children, as it would be for any Super-mom. We sat down for lunch and Phoenix, then age four, ordered first, "Caesar salad, no croutons, please, and a water." "Phoenix," I whispered, "You can order anything you want. You don't have to get a Caesar." "But Momma, it cooked," he explained sweetly. "I know, Phoenix, but you can eat anything you want on the menu from now on. You can eat anything you want. No more raw vegan." "But Momma, it cooked," he continued. "I know, love. You can eat cooked now. You can eat anything. No more labels. No more restriction."

"Grilled cheese with a side of fries!" he squealed to the waitress without skipping a beat.

That kid ate everything on his plate and just about licked it clean. And for two weeks, eating became his hobby. He'd eat three bowls of cereal with rice milk, a croissant, and a waffle for breakfast and we'd bike to the beach club where he'd announce, "Momma, I hungry" (less than an hour after breakfast). "OK," I'd say with a smile, "What do you want Hon?"

What didn't he want? He had four years to catch up on.

My mother in law is Swiss and not a fan of eating between meals, and was not amused as I said yes to his every eating desire. "Just give him time," I explained. "He just needs time."

He was eating a lot, but not eating fearfully and compulsively. He was hungry.

Sagey, age seven at the time, was the same way, but not quite as intense as Phoenix. She had eaten cooked food till she was three and I think that was the difference. She had also eaten cooked food at parties, play dates, etc. Phoenix had been raw vegan all his life.

After about two weeks Phoenix's eating calmed to a "normal roar." I think he'll always be a "good eater"—all my kids have great appetites—but now he fully understands that he can eat anything and everything that he wants now and forever.

On that fateful day—July 6, 2011—the day we decided that our kids were no longer raw vegan, I was swimming laps at our beach club and happily planning all the fun meals I was going to make my kids. "I'll make them chocolate chip pancakes every morning! I'll make stir fry veggies and tofu over brown rice! I'll make egg white omelets and home fries!" Then it hit me. "Wait a minute," I thought, "I wanna eat chocolate chip pancakes with my kids. I wanna eat stir-fry with them. I miss egg white omelets. I don't wanna be the 'weird' Mom who don't eat what her kids eat...."

"Wait a minute," I asked myself, "Did I just say, 'I miss egg white omelets?" I had never missed anything cooked the seven years we'd been raw vegan. Yet, as I swam, I recalled that the day we had arrived on Nantucket, while browsing in the Sconset Market, my eyes noticed a box of Aunt Jemima pancake mix on the shelf and I said out loud (to no one), "Those pancakes look good." The woman standing next to me laughed and said, "Yes, they do!" A coincidence? I don't believe in 'em.

I scooted back to our little rented beach house, burst into the front door, and announced to Philippe, "I am no longer raw vegan! I wanna eat chocolate chip pancakes with my kids! I wanna eat an egg while omelet! I wanna get nachos and beer with you—tonight!"

In a moment I will remember for the rest of my life, Philippe didn't skip a beat, smiled, and said, "Yeaaaahhhhhh!"

That night we all went out to dinner in town. I don't think I've ever seen my in-laws so happy as we all ordered just about everything: an egg white omelet, chocolate chip pancakes, macaroni and cheese, nachos, beer, soup, salad (yes, still salad) and so on. Thank goodness that place served breakfast 'round the clock.

I gotta say, that food tasted goooood. I tasted a little bit of everything. Then as we walked around Nantucket and shopped, I said to Philippe, "I feel fine! I don't feel sick at all."

While we were raw vegan I often said that I wished I could eat mostly raw but eat some cooked food as well since I felt it was more balanced, easier, and best for your body because your body could then handle and digest everything. Philippe and I also joked that your body would then be grateful for the really good raw vegan food when you ate it. Instead of just expecting it.

But I'd learned that my sensitive digestive system couldn't handle it. The few times I'd tried to eat cooked food (at a wedding once and when I was pregnant a few times when I had cooked food cravings) I'd been plagued with flu symptoms for weeks at worst and a pounding headache for days at best. I thought that eating raw vegan would make my digestive system stronger but it seemed to do the opposite. If I ate raw vegan I felt great, but my body couldn't handle anything else. This had always been a disappointment to me in regards to the raw vegan lifestyle, but I chalked it up to my sensitive digestion.

Well, now I felt fine after eating cooked food. No headache. No flu symptoms. Wow. The incredible power of the mind.

The next morning I still felt fine. I had some mucous in my nose from the dairy, but was unfazed. I blew my nose a few times and declared that it was worth it for those delicious nachos and the freedom to eat anything. I'm not a huge fan of cheese anyway, but from now on my motto is anything in moderation (hence the third Practice in creating the best life ever).

The weeks that followed were fun and exciting. A new time for my family and me. We were trying foods we hadn't eaten in years and Phoenix and our twin babies were eating foods they'd never eaten in their whole lifetimes.

It was also cool to see how our bodies crave and create balance. For example, the day after the first dinner out eating everything, my body craved greens and Spirulina. It wasn't a decision I'd made in my mind or a restriction; it was just what I felt like eating. The whole time I'd been raw vegan I thought that I wasn't restricting. I ate raw vegan chocolate cake and ice cream pretty much every day and reasoned that I never saw women who weren't raw vegan eating sweets like that daily (they mostly don't allow themselves to as far as I can tell). But lemme tell ya, once there was no more label, I saw that there had been restriction.

I knew by the way I felt when I was no longer a label. One word: FREE. That's the best way to describe the feeling I was enjoying and intend to enjoy from now on.

Do I still love raw vegan food?! You bet! Do I eat it all the time? Absolutely! Do I also love other cooked foods? Yes ma'am and sir!

Once I started eating everything I was surprised to learn that there had been foods I'd been missing for the last, ahem, seven years, and also surprised by what they were:

- Steamed broccoli
- Steamed spinach
- Stir-fried broccoli
- Sautéed spinach
- Eggplant cooked any way
- Stir fried mushrooms and onions
- Steamed artichokes
- Cooked tomato sauce
- Big salads with any of the above cooked veggies on top

Philippe and I laughed that I was "Mmmm Mmmmm-ing" most with steamed veggies and big salads with steamed veggies on top. "You missed steamed broccoli the most!" Philippe laughed.

I also realized that I had missed:

- Peanut Butter
- Gluten free chocolate chip pancakes
- Gluten free muffins
- True Whip
- Margaritas on the rocks with salt
- Nachos
- Gluten free pancake batter (I prefer it to the pancakes)
- Gluten free muffin batter (I prefer it to the muffins)
- Peanut butter frozen yogurt with chocolate jimmies

I thought I wasn't restricting, but as this list grew, I realized that yes, I was (unconsciously.) Because although I would eat raw vegan foods to my heart's content, including all of the desserts, the bottom line is that whenever you say "no" to something, you are including it in your vibration (according to the Law of Attraction).

I also believe that when you're grounded and in balance, your body produces whatever it needs to remain healthy and strong.

So I felt free. Something I already thought I was, but apparently not.

When we returned from Nantucket a few weeks later, the kids and I took our maiden voyage to Whole Foods. Our first time since we had stopped being a label. We spent two hours going up and down those aisles, looking at all the new things that have come out in the last seven years. There's a lot! Especially in the gluten free area. We are big fans of gluten free because we like the taste as much or more and it's easier to digest and better for you. We are not "gluten free"—no more labels—but it's fun to see what's out there now and mix it up.

That cart was soooo full and I was scared to see the total at the checkout. While raw vegan, my kids would have "ooooohed and ahhhhhed" over the watermelon, cantaloupe, apples, and grapes, but now mumbled, "No thanks" when I suggested we buy some produce. I let it go. I wanted to give them time.

I felt free.

That ginormous cart of food cost half what our food used to cost when we were raw vegan. Shows you how much cheaper processed foods are, which is a big problem for the health of our country. No restriction, but balance is key. Everyone should be able to afford to buy fresh produce.

The second time we went to Whole Foods we were in and out in fifteen minutes. Kinda like Phoenix stopped eating 24/7 after a few weeks.

We've now been living label-free for about a year and I feel great. I actually have more energy than ever and I chalk that up to one thing: freedom. Freedom=Prana=Joy=Energy.

My body has become stronger and better able to handle anything. I can eat anything in moderation and feel great. I can even drink margaritas, which I did at my birthday dinner at an authentic Mexican restaurant that my friends own. Them were some strong margaritas, and

I awoke the next morning with... no hangover. I'm not advocating alcohol consumption per se, but everything you love, in moderation.

After seven years of living a raw vegan lifestyle, I feel that the means had become the end. Raw food was supposed to make us healthier and stronger but in the end it became the end. It became a prison. In fact, our bodies became more sensitive and needed foods to be prepared "just so" to feel optimal.

This was annoying and restricting at best. We thought we'd be super human digesters, like when you work out and get strong and have more endurance, but it didn't work the same way with our digestive systems. In the end our bodies couldn't handle anything but super clean raw vegan food. And then it's not a choice. It's a must. And that's a prison.

Anything can become a prison. Zen living can even become a prison if you must do this, this, and that. In the end, it's supposed to be a tool and you're supposed to be able to go beyond the "rules."

In the end, anything you're doing to enhance your life and create the best life ever is supposed to be a tool and you're supposed to be able to go beyond "the rules." You're supposed to be able to be flexible. To have balance and moderation. And choice. This is freedom.

It's all about balance. We had always said to our students, consulting clients, and friends to "add in" and do as much raw vegan as they wanted to, that it wasn't about being a label or being 100% raw vegan, unless they specifically wanted that, and even then, I would ask if that was really what they wanted. I explained to them that I had always wished I could play the edge and eat mostly raw and some cooked foods, but my body "wouldn't let me."

In the end I learned that it was my mind that wouldn't let me, and my physicality then backed up my beliefs. I got myself one strong mind, as do you. Anything is possible, if you believe.

My body is now thanking me for this lifestyle change. It's wicked grateful when I give it green juice, for example. After drinking three green juices every morning for years, I went cold turkey with no green juice for over two months because I'd given away my juicer when we built our restaurant (which we sold in the fall of 2011) and I just didn't feel like getting another. Instead I ate a lotta Spirulina, which I craved and was much easier to get my hands on than green juice.

Now I'm drinking green juice again when I feel like it and my body is so thankful, soaking it up like a sponge. But I'm not freaked out if green juice isn't available. The panic is gone. A panic I didn't even know was there. It takes a lot of energy to panic! All that energy now goes to creating the best life ever. Manifesting my dreams.

I've noticed too that when I drink green juice it balances out when I eat something not quite as healthy. It's all about balance. And gratitude. And I have multiplied these two things in my life since deciding not to be a label anymore. It took making a huge lifestyle change and facing my fear in service of and to my five children.

Have my kids grown more and faster since eating everything? Hell yeah. Sagey (now age eight) grew two inches in the first two weeks after letting go of the label. Phoenix (age four at the time) grew 1.5 inches. They filled out more and still love a good Caesar salad and smoothie.

We still offer our kids "balance" with every meal (a raw fruit or veggie). But there ain't no more restriction.

The twins started walking almost immediately after the lifestyle switch and have been growing like weeds ever since, moving from the 3rd percentile to the 53rd percentile in just seven months. Who knows if the walking was due to the food. I'm just sayin.'

When I was anorexic in college it felt like my world kept getting smaller. Can't eat this. Can't do that. Can't drink this. Can't do that. Eventually I had so many rules it was stifling. A prison. In the end, the label of 100% raw vegan became a prison as well.

I don't believe in mistakes or regret. I'm grateful to the Universe that we were able to walk the raw vegan path, learn our lessons, and fork in a different direction immediately when the intuition arose. I'm so grateful that my children are now so healthy and strong, growing well, and loving all types of foods. I'm grateful that we are all now truly free and that from this learning, the third Practice of creating the best life ever was born.

# Chapter 9

# The Manifestation

"You create your own Universe as you go along."
- Winston Churchill

The Universe is always giving us gifts. Always. But are your eyes open to see them? Can you see and allow what you've created with your thoughts, words, emotions, and actions?

When I had the ultrasound confirming that I was, indeed, having twins, my good friend Dianne offered to watch Sagey (age 5 at the time) and Phoenix (age 2 at the time) on Thursday mornings for a few hours "so you can rest on the couch, Taylor, and put some meat on those bones!" (Said in the most amazing Irish accent you can imagine).

One Thursday morning, as I was dropping off the kids at Dianne's, I drove by the most beautiful house I'd ever seen. It was, in fact, a white castle. I said out loud to my kiddos, "Oh my goodness, that's the prettiest house I've ever seen. I wanna buy it." My kids giggled in the back seat, and exclaimed that it was, indeed, a castle (or "cattil" in two-year-old Phoenix-speak).

After finishing my practice at the Pink House (as we and others affectionately called our home, named after its oh-so-bright pink color), I called Philippe to ask if he could pick up the kids from

Dianne's house. I was exhausted from being pregnant with twins and needed to rest. He drove by the same house, said the exact same words, the kids giggled, and on they went.

Fast forward to the next day. Philippe said to me, "There's a house for sale a few doors up from Dianne." "Oh I know, I wanna buy that house, it's a white castle," I replied matter-of-factly. "Me too!" Philippe exclaimed. "Let's buy it," I said with an air of confidence that's evident when something is a "done deal." We smiled at each other in the same way that we smiled when I had an epiphany on my mat ten years before and said to (my then boyfriend) Philippe, "We're

## The Universe is always giving us gifts.

going to open a yoga studio and it's called Prana Power Yoga," and he said, without a pause and very matter-of-factly, "OK." Three months later we opened our first Prana Power Yoga studio in Newton Corner and we've opened four more Prana Power Yoga studios since. When things are lined up, they're lined up. When they're meant to happen, they're meant to happen. But I digress....

Two days later we saw the White Castle on the inside (it was Yom Kippur so the seller's real estate agent didn't call me back for two days). Within twenty seconds of stepping into it I said to the seller's agent, "I'm like no buyer you've ever met. I don't play games. I don't mess around. I'm extremely honest and up front. We're going to buy this house. It is, in fact, our house. So you can stop showing it. It's a done deal."

She paused for about five seconds and then said that she'd like to do a consulting session with me since she'd never met anyone like me before. I laughed and immediately began giving her suggestions ("You gotta get off dairy, Sister, and about that soy...").

We bought the house—done deal—eight days later.

In a real estate market that's not friendly toward entrepreneurs who put just about every dollar that comes into their yoga studios back into their yoga studios (and had just built a restaurant) saying that this manifestation was a miracle is somewhat of an understatement.

The things that lined up—quickly and efficiently—for this deal to go through with remarkable ease and speed confirmed everything I've ever read, taught, and lived about Deliberate Creation and manifesting what you want in your life.

We weren't looking for a new house. We loved our Pink House, our yard, our neighborhood, our neighbors. This house found us, and the energy that propelled us to buy it was incredibly powerful. There was simply no resistance, in any way, shape, or form.

Our real estate agent said on more than one occasion, "I've never seen anything like this. No deals go this way." She is now practicing at Prana.

The details of how it went down are private, but I will tell you that the night we were waiting for the sellers to get back to us on our offer... waiting, waiting... I noticed that I had posted the following quote on my Super-mom.com blog for that very day. I had queued this quote to be posted on this particular day way before I'd laid eyes on the white castle:

Super-Quote of the Day, Tuesday October 6, 2009:

> "Waiting for the fish to bite or waiting for wind to fly a kite. Or waiting around for Friday night or waiting perhaps for their Uncle Jake or a pot to boil or a better break or a string of pearls or a pair of pants or a wig with curls or another chance. Everyone is just waiting."
> — Dr. Seuss, Oh! The Places You'll Go!

(The Seller's name was Jake).

I sat stunned as I read the quote that chilly autumn evening, and called Philippe to the computer. He read it and was speechless for a moment, and then said "That's God. That's proof of God."

We almost never use the "G word" in our studios or when we teach elsewhere or even in our home because it's so triggering for so many people for so many reasons, so when he said this, it was powerful.

I had posted the Dr. Seuss quote (and the accompanying article) about six months prior. Coincidence? I don't believe in 'em. Just synchronicities, divinely sent.

The day that we first saw the inside of the White Castle, I was listening to Abraham-Hicks on my iPod, and "happened" to hear a man asking what to do when "you want something finite—like a house or a car or to win a lottery—and you really think you're going to get it, and you don't?"

Abraham-Hicks said that there was one big flaw in his thinking. He was talking about something finite and the Universe is infinite. She said that it's best to find the essence of what you want and go for that, not for one specific thing.

At this point I was thinking, "Forget that! I want the White Castle! It's our house!" Abraham-Hicks then said that there's one exception—when you absolutely positively have a knowing that something is yours. There's no doubt. There's no fear. It just is.

"That's more like it, Sister!" I smiled as I brushed my teeth and kept listening. Then she said something that again made me pause and actually sit down because of its power.

Abraham-Hicks asked the man if he'd ever experienced a situation where he wasn't asking or looking for something and it came—FAST—and then he realized that a long, long time ago, he'd asked for it in some way, shape, or form.

"Oh my God!" I thought to myself, as I recalled being eighteen and visiting my parents while on holiday break from Brown. They were penniless and living in a construction site. My dad's friend had "given them a break" by giving him the job of "managing" the construction of a condo complex while living in the one condo that was semi-finished. My parents had no furniture. I slept on the floor as construction noises woke me at the crack of dawn—not the usual schedule of a freshman in college.

I didn't fret, I didn't complain, I didn't feel sorry for my parents or myself. Instead, I visualized where I'd live one day—someplace very, very different than my current circumstances. And I found things to be happy about. I found things to be grateful for.

I'd go for walks in an affluent part of Dallas called Highland Park and look at those beautiful homes with joy. What beautiful architecture! And I'd send light to those so blessed to live there. I felt so happy for them and what they had created, and experienced joy from just looking at the beauty they'd manifested.

There was one particular home that was my favorite. I'd stop in front of it and stare at it for a while. It looked like a white castle. "One day," I proclaimed, "I will live in a white castle."

Fast-forward twenty-six years. We were moving into a white castle.

I had totally forgotten about the white castle in Highland Park, Texas, until I heard the Abraham-Hicks CD. I had forgotten about the rocket of desire I had launched over two and a half decades before. But the Universe had not.

The Universe had been lining things up for me—oh so carefully—so that when the White Castle came into my life, there really wasn't anything I could do to screw up the deal. All I had to do was follow my heart, and believe. Which, at this point, after so many yoga practices, is easy for me.

Whatever you want, whatever you're wishing for—the Universe hears you. It's coming. At the perfect time and in the perfect way. All you need to do is ask, and allow. This is Deliberate Creation. The second Practice of creating the best life ever.

# Chapter 10

# The Haters

*"It is the combination of thought and love which forms the irresistible force of the Law of Attraction."*
*- Charles Haanel*

I don't like the word "hate." I think it's one of the worst of the four letter words (right behind d-i-e-t), and I don't allow it in our home.

I notice that people use this word a lot and, unbeknownst to them, it's creating their future and their life, one word at a time. Even if they say something as "innocuous" as "I hate waiting in lines" or "I hate Mondays," or other such accepted clichés, watch out! That's one powerful word.

I suggest to my children, consulting clients, students, readers, friends, and family to say instead what it is that you like or love: "I love the weekends" or "I like Wednesdays because the work week is half over" or "I love when lines move really quickly" or "I love when I can meditate or visualize cool things that I want while waiting in a long line."

So to name this chapter "The Haters" and write that word even once is not the norm for me. I chose to address this phenomenon (the "hater" mentality) to give you some tools with which to approach any "hater situation" in which you may find yourself. I hope you find yourself in none and these tools are unnecessary, but you'll have 'em just in case .

If you listen closely, you'll notice that those in the public eye who reach many people with their work address "the haters" on a regular basis. Will Smith has a line in one of his songs that says, "No love for the haters, the haters, mad 'cause I have floor seats at the Lakers."

Sean Croxton says while looking straight at the camera in one of his YouTube videos about detoxing, "Haters, get your pens out, here it is, my recommendation."

Because Philippe and I are super-blessed and magnetize the nicest people ever to Prana Power Yoga, I hadn't had a lot of experience with "the haters." I can count on one hand the number of "difficult" students I've encountered over ten years of teaching at Prana.

After describing a manifestation in my life on my Super-mom.com blog (the manifestation I told you about in Chapter 9) and explaining how to create the same type of manifestations in your life, I had my first real taste of "the haters."

I was taken aback. It hurt to have people say things with such negative energy and misunderstand my intentions and me so dramatically. As I read the words, I felt as though someone had punched me in the stomach. I was surprised, stunned, and confused.

"Was that their intention?" I wondered. "To make me feel negative energy?" That's certainly what I was feeling.

My mind went back in time to two of my teachers' comments about me needing to "have a thicker skin" and to "stop being so naïve and 'airy-fairy'—always thinking and believing in the best in people."

"Maybe they were right," I thought in my temporarily wounded state. I thought about throwing in the towel—bagging my Super-mom.com blog all together. I had started it about two years prior to spread light, love, inspiration, and support, and to create much-needed community; and these "haters" were slamming me.

But with time, reflection, and meditation, my Warrior Spirit was revived, and I was back.

As my good friend Cita said to me in one of the many supportive emails and posts I received after "the haters" posted on my Super-mom.com blog, "Taylor you have never changed your behavior based on others, and don't you dare start now! It's one of the things that I love and respect about you. It's what makes you you and it's what inspires me to believe in myself more during times of self-doubt. There will always be haters, for lack of a better word, but really that's what they are. They choose to see the dark side. But their darkness has nothing to do with the absolute beauty and goodness that is you. Of course they got you down. That was their intent. And they probably LOVE that they got you down. But at the end of the day, they have to move through life looking at everything that way—through a dark lens—and boy, is that an exhausting, defeating way of looking at life."

This got me to thinking about "the haters." How did they come to hate as they do, and why do they choose to project their negative energy onto other well-meaning people who usually don't see it coming? I asked the Universe, as I often do, "What's the lesson here? What do I need to learn? What do I need to do differently?"

My warrior spirit was revived.

And the answer came.

"The haters" are afraid. As Marianne Williamson said, in any situation, there is only love or fear. If you're not choosing love, you're choosing fear.

When people are mean, they are afraid. When people are rude, they are afraid. When people are closed-minded, they are afraid. When people are judgmental, they are afraid. When people "hate," they are afraid.

What to do?

Be aware. Breathe. Stay calm. Be non-reactive. Don't take it personally. Send them light. Send them love. And ignore it as best as you can. Remember, it's all about the power of the focus of your mind. Focus on something else.

You may think I've lost my mind. "Why on earth would I send someone so nasty light and love?" you ask, and quite rightly so.

Because they need it. Because the planet needs it. Because that is actually what they're asking for. To react to them—to send more hate their way—is a fast track to the dark side yourself.

Can you stay calm in a difficult moment? It's easy to love the loves—the gems. But can you love the haters? I know it's a challenge. Or even more challenging than that.

But to teach the hater that you are light and love no matter what may shift them. Or maybe not. Whether or not they hear or feel a word you are saying, you have prevailed because you haven't shifted yourself to a dark place to which you never intended on going (and where they reside).

So if you are ever approached, attacked or slammed by a "hater," go on wit yo' bad self and shine your light. Know that their words and actions are not about you. But you choosing the light is.

Chapter 11

# It's Never Too Early or Too Late

Take a deep breath in and a deep breath out. It'll be all right because it's NEVER too late to begin again.

It's never too early or too late. To start yoga. To wake up. To begin again.

## To start yoga:

Above is a photo of our son Phoenix at fourteen-months-old practicing yoga. He started his practice in my belly while I was pregnant and practicing daily.

I've noticed that when people see little ones practicing yoga, they often comment "Wow, imagine what life would've been like if I'd started then …."

It's never too early, but it's never too late, either. Philippe met a seventy-seven-year-old yogi on a retreat once. He was the healthiest, most vibrant, and most flexible person on the trip. He was a self-proclaimed "late bloomer," beginning his practice at age sixty-five.

## To wake up:

I started waking up at 4 am when I stopped being a label. For my whole life, I've been fascinated and inspired by early-wakers. "How DO they do it?" I wondered in awe and with deep respect because I was a "night owl," finding it easy to stay up till the wee hours—not wake up in the wee hours.

Then something just clicked a while back and I made a decision, set an intention, and… set an alarm. I had been waking up really early over the weekend prior to practice before teaching our Prana Power Yoga Teacher Training, so I figured it was a good time to start. I had momentum!

Now I wake with ease and no alarm at 4 am, feeling refreshed, rested, and excited for the new day. The secret? Practice. That's all it took. Like anything else, really. This thing that had fascinated, inspired, and scared me a bit for so many years wasn't so hard after all. And now it's my favorite time of day… so quiet, so peaceful, and so full of promise.

Another type of "waking up" that it's never too late to do is waking up to the NOW, to this moment, to the awareness that brings you back to who you are. Why you are on this planet. Best way to do this by far (in my humble opinion)? Get on your yoga mat. The three Practices for creating The Best Life Ever flow together seamlessly.

## To begin again:

You've had "that" moment, "that" day, "that" week, "that" year. Things have not gone as you'd hoped and planned. You acted out, missed out, lost out, and generally behaved in a way that is not the best representation of your authentic self.

Yoga teaches us to see the truth. One truth I've learned through my practice is that it's never too late to begin again. All it takes is awareness ("This is not working, this feels bad, I want to begin again.") and intention ("My intention is to have a fresh start right now"). Sound too simple to be true? Most things do.

# Chapter 12

# The Transformation

*"There is nothing that cannot happen today."*
*- Mark Twain*

When I was thirty-two, I had my first daughter, Madison. It was a day that changed me forever. I would never be the same.

I loved being a Super-mom more than anything, but told my husband in no uncertain terms that I wanted to wait at least three years before even talking about having another child.

Two and three-quarters years later, I found a tabloid under our guest room bed. I giggled as I flipped through it (my husband was embarrassed he'd bought it and so he had hidden it), and through my laughter, a headline caught my eye: "Madonna: Pregnant and Lovin' It." The headline that would change my life forever.

The article talked about how Madonna was having a great pregnancy because she was practicing yoga. She'd had a rough go of it during her first pregnancy, it explained, with nausea, vomiting, and intense fatigue, but this time around was different, thanks to the yoga. I, too, had had nausea 24/7 for twenty-six weeks of my pregnancy with Madison, and had thrown up about twenty times a day.

Off I went to my first yoga class.

So off I went to my first yoga class. As I rolled up my mat at the end of my practice, I said to myself with joy, "This is it! This is what I've been looking for! This is my Dharma." I had no idea I'd been "looking for" anything. But now I'd found it.

My only concern was how I was going to fit this practice in every day. I was in an intense doctoral program in clinical psychology and had a young child. But my Spirit had spoken.

So fit it in I did—daily, and sometimes twice a day, waking up at 5 am so I could practice before my daughter woke up and then practicing again in a 5:45 pm class at a studio.

The most amazing thing to me was that I could receive so much from a 60-90 minute practice—total calm, focus, energy, joy, spiritual connection, and the best workout ever. I had never come close to this experience during a lifetime of competitive sports, beginning at age five as a competitive figure skater and continuing when I played tennis competitively and trained with Nick Bollettieri to go pro.

Six weeks later I was in Chatham, Massachusetts at a Fourth of July celebration, surrounded by balloons, a band, a gazebo, and hoards of (very preppy, wealthy, conservative) people. I felt like I was in a daze. I stared at my surroundings and asked myself, "What IS this? What have I created? This is so not me, and I created it in my life." I felt totally alone, although I was surrounded by tons of people. I felt as though I couldn't breathe—like I was in a prison, with no freedom. I will remember that moment for the rest of my life.

My husband noticed that I was "off" and asked me if I was OK. "I'm just confused... just looking for some clarity," I responded quietly.

Clarity I got. Ask and you shall receive. Three weeks later, after practicing yoga for only nine weeks, I went on my first yoga retreat. I jetted off to Montana to seek the clarity that my Spirit had asked for. I practiced yoga six hours a day, cried for just about as many hours, hiked in the mountains, ate clean vegetarian food, and let go.

Yoga lifts the veils of illusion and my practice gave me the biggest gifts ever—truth, clarity, and courage. I returned home and my husband and I separated two weeks later, something that had needed to happen for many years.

Two weeks later, on my birthday, I was filming a yoga video for one of my yoga teachers and the producer moved me away from my "regular" spot to the other side of the room. As I laid down my mat, I glanced to my right and my mouth dropped open in awe, "Oh my God!" I said to the student next to me, "I had a dream about you last night!"

I had indeed had a dream about this person whom I had never seen before, and I've never been one to beat around the bush or hold back words.

As I looked at him, time stood still. It was uncanny. Everyone else in the room disappeared. He responded—not skipping a beat—with, "So I am, quite literally, the man of your dreams."

And that was it. For our Spirits anyway.

It took me awhile to actually let Philippe into my heart, even though my Spirit recognized him in that very first instant as my soul mate.

I had recently been separated, and was not looking for love in any way, shape, or form. I had decided that I had loved once, was blessed to have done so, and was going to be a "happy, single Mom" and raise my daughter solo.

So after that fateful first meeting, I avoided Philippe when I saw him at the yoga studio. He'd say "Hi" and we'd talk briefly and then I'd find a way to steal away as quickly as I could. Fear was over-ruling my heart.

Several months later, Philippe and I went on our first date to a Dharma talk at The Insight Meditation Center in Cambridge, Massachusetts. I smiled at the irony. My first date with my ex-husband had been to a frat party at Brown and my first date with Philippe was to a Dharma talk at The Cambridge Insight Meditation Center. We listened, meditated, and then talked in the car afterward for three hours.

We've been together ever since.

I felt totally alone. I felt as though I couldn't breathe like I was in a prison, with no freedom.

People frequently ask me how we met and I love telling the story. I love seeing the surprise and joy in people's eyes regarding how incredibly "lined up" our meeting was. Not lined up by Philippe or me or Match.com. Lined up by the Universe. In perfect order.

But what if the producer hadn't moved me? What if I'd refused to move?

Yoga lifts the veils of illusion and my practice gave me the biggest gifts ever—truth, clarity, and courage.

I'm asked these questions often, and my answer is always the same. If you are surrendered enough to let the Universe create its miracles, the miracles will come. At the perfect time. And at record speed. When you cultivate and utilize your yoga and Deliberate Creation Practices on a regular basis and allow the miracles to come by offering no resistance in any way, it's a slam-dunk.

Two and a half years after our fateful meeting we opened our first Prana Power Yoga Studio in Newton, Massachusetts. A month after that we moved into a pink house with my daughter Madison, then age four. Two months later we got married in the front yard of our pink house. Seven months after that we filmed our first Prana Power Yoga DVD. The day after filming our DVD, I became pregnant with Sage, now eight-years-old.

Since that day, we have had three more children (Phoenix, age five; Dakota, age two; and Montana, age two); opened four more Prana Power Yoga studios (in Brooklyn, New York; Cambridge, Massachusetts; Winchester, Massachusetts; and Union Square, New York); launched Super-mom.com; created The Prana Cleanse™; opened and later sold a raw vegan restaurant; and created Prana Super-mom Consulting.

The creation and the joy that are possible when you are lined up, allow the flow of the Universe, and listen to your heart are never-ending and abundant. Just keep cultivating and utilizing the three Practices. Make it fun. Keep visualizing what's coming to inspire you to stay on track. And be light about it. Be easy. Be playful. Don't take it or yourself too seriously. It's supposed to be fun!

As I let go a little bit more every morning on my yoga mat, more of the magic of the Universe flows into my moment-to-moment experience. The miracles keep coming and they're gaining momentum. It can be like this for you too. It will be like this for you too, as you consistently utilize the three Practices of creating the best life ever. If you are surrendered and open to the divine flow of The Universe, the day will come when you just have to think a thought—just think about something that you want—and it will manifest instantly. So stay on the path. And remember, if it's taking time, it's getting even better and even more specific.

# Chapter 13

# "The One"

*"To acquire love...fill yourself up with
it until you become a magnet."*
*- Charles Haanel*

How many times have you heard this question, "Is he (or she) 'the one?'"

Most likely you've heard this question at least once before. What exactly does it mean? How do you know if he or she is "the one?"

Philippe and I want all the same things in life, but we never once talked about these things before we got married. Never once discussed how many children each of us wanted to have, how we wanted to raise our children, if we wanted to travel, where we wanted to travel, how we wanted to travel, where we wanted to live...the list goes on. But we did know one thing—our Spirits wanted to be together. When we were together, it felt like "home," like a "done deal" from very early on in our relationship. There was no decision to make—we were destined to be together.

Only now, ten years, five children and five yoga studios later, are we stopping for a moment and saying, "Wow we are so blessed that we want all the same things in life because since we do, things flow easily and joyfully on our path."

We weren't operating from our minds when we came together. We were operating from our hearts. And look what happened. Everything lined up perfectly.

A lesson in creating your best life ever, utilizing the three Practices. Let the Universe take care of the details. Just follow your heart and let go.

# Chapter 14

# Why I Practice Asana

# Yoga is a commitment to being your authentic self.

As I laid my baby boy in his crib and he let out a little whimper and sigh as he settled deeply into sleep, time stood still and everything became clear and simple. A love that is almost indescribable filled my entire being—body, mind, and Spirit.

I stood there for a few minutes gazing at my baby's plump little body enveloped in his mint green snuggle suit, his perfectly round head with just a whisper of blonde hair, and savored the love, the energy, and the Prana that flowed through my entire self. I opened up my palms and felt the light and love pour in. This is the essence of love. This is the essence of life.

This is why I practice yoga day in and day out, asana (Sanskrit for "pose") after asana, sweaty towel after sweaty towel. To be able to truly open my heart and Spirit, and savor this moment of pure love. In years past—years prior to my discipline, my dharma, my life of yoga—I would have been unable to truly savor this moment. To truly feel life and time standing still. To realize that this is it! This is the only moment that matters. And a love so divine is all that I am here to experience.

Prior to my yogic path, I would have been off to the next thing—the dishes, writing another post or book chapter, the laundry, a hundred unread emails, uploading the latest photos of the kids, editing the latest email blast, the architectural and lighting plans for the next studio. But because I practice asana day after day, I am able to be truly present for and in this precious moment. I am able to not miss it—to not miss my life.

Someone once said to not be afraid of dying, but to be afraid of not living. As I walk around in our world, I see a lot of people asleep. Asleep to the joy of life, asleep to the miracles happening every single moment, asleep to the love surrounding all of us. I see a lot of people not living. I see a lot of people focused on the darkness, the fear, the drama, the gossip, the next thing. Missing the fact that a happy life is just a string of happy moments, but most people don't allow the happy moment because they are so busy trying to get a happy life.

But it doesn't dishearten me. Because my asana keeps me living in the light, and focused on the light. I see the pure potential in every single being with whom I come into contact. Even with all the distraction of daily life—all the stimuli coming at each and every one of us constantly—I imagine them after only one yoga practice, already starting to lift the veils of illusion, already starting to melt the ice around their beautiful heart, already beginning to awaken. Awaken to their life, awaken to their light, awaken to this moment. Exactly as it is in all its simplicity and beauty.

I see the light in them that is in every single one of us. No matter how lost, how fearful, how angry, how sad. My asana helps me to see the light, to spread the light and to endlessly, tirelessly, and joyfully inquire, "Would you like to take a free class at my yoga studio?"

One practice is all it takes.

Chapter 15

# The Birth

This is a metaphor for life. In those moments when you feel you can't go on, stay on the path, believe in yourself, and breathe.

When I had my first baby, I was clueless about the birthing process. Of course I was clueless! I'd never done it before. I had Madison (now fourteen) after thirty-six hours—twenty-nine hours of natural labor followed by an epidural, four more hours of waiting to dilate, pitocin to help me to dilate since it wasn't a-happenin', and then two hours and fifteen minutes of pushing.

Ouch!

Sagey (now eight) came after nine hours total. Six hours of natural labor followed by an epidural and eventually the pushing—the duration of which I can't recall.

Then came Phoenix (now five). Phoenix's birth was three hours, all natural, and two pushes. I brought him into the world while squatting in malasana (squat pose) and in total silence, eyes closed, and hands in "namaste." I refused to get into a bed and my midwife accommodated me. As well she should! Remember Super-moms, it's your birthing experience. Be in your power!

Philippe's sister Jennifer gave me the best advice ever before Phoenix's birth. She said to visualize the pain as a red ball in my belly and focus on it during the whole contraction, breathing into it. She told me to keep the focus and not get distracted. I'd tried everything else in births one and two, so I was open to trying anything. And it made sense to me.

So with the beginning of each contraction with Phoenix, I set a timer and breathed Ujjayi breath as I closed my eyes and focused on the red ball of pain in my belly. And it worked! As long as I had total silence in the room. Once Philippe started to ask me something during a painful contraction while I was focusing, and I totally lost my focus on "the red ball of pain" and the pain became unbearable. Let's just say he didn't do THAT again.

After three hours, I had the contraction of all contractions. The contraction that didn't end. One minute, two minutes, three minutes, four minutes, five minutes...yes, five minutes of excruciating pain with no end in sight. As I journeyed into minute five, I blurted out, "I want an epidural!" to my doula, Philippe, and my midwife, who'd just walked in the room (she mostly left us alone for the whole time, which was what we wanted). "OK, Taylor...we need to hook you up to an IV first, and then we need to . . ." my midwife began. "NO! I want an epidural now!" I interrupted while dealing as best I could with the continuing pain of the contraction from Hell.

"Let me just check you," my midwife soothed. "Oh! No, no epidural, Taylor, the head is right there!" She continued. "We just need to break your water." I pushed as hard as I could and my water broke—all over my midwife. Philippe cheered. All I remember then is my midwife saying, "Don't push!" I ignored her, pushed with all of my might, and out came baby Phoenix, perfect and healthy and beautiful. Someone said, "Atta girl!" (to me) and someone else said, "It's a baby boy!" and so I asked out loud, "Is it a girl or a boy?"

PHOTO: PHYLLIS GORMAN

The answer was clear in a second as my son was laid on my chest. No words could ever describe the magic and the power of giving birth. It hurts like nothing you've ever felt (unless you've had kids, then you know what I'm talking about, Super-moms) but man, that feeling—that feeling of just giving birth. If I could bottle it....

And the unmistakable feeling of "I can do anything!" after it's all over. The incredible feeling of, "If I did that, I can do anything!" Talk about empowering. No matter how your birthing experience flows. I'm a big believer in "whatever it takes, Super-moms!" Whatever it takes to deliver your baby (or babies) to the world safely and healthfully. There is no "good" or "bad" labor and delivery— no judgment. Drugs. No drugs. Vaginal. C-section. Whatever! Every birth experience is different and beautiful in its own way. Be proud of your birth experience(s) for what they were—a divine miracle.

All four of my labors and deliveries were wonderful and magical in their own ways. I didn't know about the squat position for my first two births (helloooow, gravity) and that helped a lot with Phoenix's birth, as did my sister-in-law's amazing advice regarding focus. My twins' mandatory C-section was divinely sent. I'll tell you more about that in Chapter 28.

It's common to hear that it's "impossible" for a person with a trauma history to have an all-natural birthing experience. Don't listen to that, Super-people, because anything is possible. Anything. If you believe, and incorporate the three Practices into your daily life.

Just when I felt I couldn't take the pain anymore and asked for an epidural with Phoenix, I pushed through, believed in him and myself, and I did it.

This is a metaphor for life. In those moments when you feel you can't go on, stay on the path, believe in yourself, and breathe.

# Chapter 16

# The Stick

*"It takes no time for the Universe to manifest what you want. Any time delay you experience is due to your delay in getting to the place of believing, knowing, and feeling that you already have it. It is you getting yourself on the frequency of what you want. When you are on that frequency, then what you want will appear."*
*- The Secret*

When Phoenix (now five) was a toddler I thought I was pregnant with my fourth child. Philippe and I had set our intention to have another baby, we visualized (utilizing Deliberate Creation) and we "tried." I felt queasy, tired, starving, bloated, and, well, just pregnant. My breasts were sore. I felt "different." Smells of certain foods began to bother me. I knew I was. I KNEW I was! I got really excited. I waited. And I waited. And after two weeks, I did the test.

And there it was—the stick. That little piece of plastic that holds the answer to a dream and manifestation come true or a sad pit in your stomach that's difficult to put into words.

It was negative.

I didn't believe it. "I've tested too early," I assured myself. I waited a few more days and tested again. For my first three children I'd gotten false negatives. The pregnancy tests showed a negative because I tested "too early." I put quotation marks around "too early" because although I waited the "standard" two weeks, my body needs about three to give me the thumbs up.

But also for every one of my first three children, I'd gotten "true negatives"—negative pregnancy tests when I truly thought—I KNEW—I was pregnant, but wasn't.

I've talked to countless Super-moms about this syndrome and we all concur: there is something that happens the month or two before you actually conceive which emulates pregnancy. The symptoms are real and palpable. My friend who's an energy healer and acupuncturist swears that this is the body and Spirit's way of preparing to create a life.

It is, after all, the most important creation there is (in my humble opinion.) It's cool and fun to create other stuff—a yoga studio, a computer program, a film, a book, a website, a batch of muffins, an article, a beautiful space to live in, a blog, a craft with your kids, a garden, an academic degree, etc. The list of what we can create is endless! And that in and of itself is amazing and wondrous. Ponder that for just a moment: the list of what you and I can create is limited only by our minds. And if you utilize the three Practices of creating the best life ever, you can and will create quickly and effortlessly. Pretty amazing.

But nothing compares to creating new life, so doesn't it make sense that there is some "more" preparation in order? More than just "trying" and conceiving—possibly only minutes later? What other action in your life can shift your life irrevocably in one instant—forever? Doesn't it make sense that The Universe sets it up so that the path is cleared a bit—prepared energetically so to speak—before this profound shift happens?

But what about those who never have this experience—feeling they are pregnant before they actually are? Are they not as "in tune" with their bodies and Spirits as those who do have this experience? Or is this not real? Is it only that some Super-moms (myself included) create psychosomatic symptoms to emulate pregnancy because we want it so much? It's been documented many a time—the woman who visits her doctor swearing she's pregnant, with a swollen belly and many symptoms (most of which are not enjoyable) to prove it. But there's no baby.

So I did the test. And the stick was...negative. I felt surprised, but not really. I guess a part of me knew I wasn't pregnant, even though I really felt I was.

Many, many hours on my yoga mat and studying Deliberate Creation came in handy because I felt disappointed and sad for only a moment. Then I was back into excited and anticipatory mode. I had faith and knew that our fourth baby, Dakota, was coming, and would come at the perfect time.

# Chapter 17

# The Coincidence

PHOTO: KELLY LORENZ

## The Universe is always giving you clues, so pay attention.

I don't believe in coincidences. I believe in synchronicities, divinely inspired and a beautiful indication that you're on the right path. The more you practice utilizing the three Practices of creating the best life ever, the more synchronicities will show up in your life. The more you practice yoga, Deliberate Creation, and the incredible freedom of eating whatever you love in moderation, the more synchronicities will appear "out of nowhere." The more the three Practices become a way of life for you, the more your life will resemble a fun and exciting adventure and mystery with clues unfolding each moment.

A few weeks after I had gotten a big negative on "the stick" I had my bi-monthly thyroid blood work done and asked them to test for pregnancy. That test was also negative. The weekend after that test Philippe leaned over and whispered to me during a Prana Power Yoga Teacher Training session, "I saw a rabbit in our yard this morning." We, both believed that when we saw a rabbit it was a sign from the Universe that I was pregnant. I smiled even though I "knew" that this wasn't "our month" for Project Dakota coming to fruition because the pregnancy test at the doctor's office had been negative.

The following week Philippe handed me a business card. "Look what I found!" he said with a smile. It was my midwife's card—a good three years old—that had somehow re-surfaced from under a pillow on the playroom couch. "It's a sign!" He exclaimed. "Just like the rabbit!" "Yes, it's a sign," I sighed with a smile, loving the synchronicities of the baby waiting to come to us, but still waiting for the actual physical manifestation to make its way into our lives.

The following Monday it snowed. The kids had no school and my chiropractor canceled my weekly appointment, so we didn't do the ultrasound work on my lower back that we do to open it up—a procedure you'd never do if you were pregnant.

On Friday after I taught the noontime class at Prana Newton, a student asked if I was pregnant. "No," I said. "I did a blood test at the doctor's and it was negative."

"Hmmm, that's weird," she replied. "I could've sworn you were and I'm usually right on. But I guess no one's right 100% of the time."

The next afternoon another student told me she had dreamt I was pregnant. "Some day soon," I smiled.

Meanwhile, my breasts were sore, my low back ached, I was starving all the time, I had mild cramping in my abdomen, and was heading to bed every night exhausted right after I put my three kids down. "PMS," I told myself, as my period was one, two, three...nine, ten, eleven days late.

No matter what the Universe sent my way in the form of divine messages (synchronicities) that Baby Dakota was indeed in my belly, I was not open to this information. The blood test had spoken. It's very important to be open to the divine messages from the Universe as they are sent to you, in order to manifest the best life ever, utilizing the three Practices. Sometimes—oftentimes—things appear in ways we are not expecting.

How many messages and synchronicities do we miss because we aren't open? Because someone or something or an "authority" has told us otherwise? How much life and joy are we closed down to, even if messages are coming from our very own bodies? And how do we open up to these magical messages? This adventurous fun and mystery? It's super-simple: slow down, breathe, and connect.

For me, the easiest and most enjoyable way to do this is to get on my yoga mat daily. My practice keeps me connected to the magic and the joy that is all around me every moment, when I'm present enough to be open to it.

Sure there are still times when I miss it—the magical message—(I was seven weeks pregnant when the student asked if I was, but was "sure" that I wasn't), but I'm on the path. And so are you. By reading this chapter, this book, and including the three Practices of creating the best life ever into your life as often as possible.

# Chapter 18

# The Surprise

"At the moment of commitment,
the Universe conspires to assist you."
- Goethe

One mid March morning in 2009 I woke up early, peed in a cup to do a pregnancy test, and got on my yoga mat.

After my practice I woke up my three kiddos, got them ready for school, fed them the best breakfast ever, and was helping them get their coats, boots, hats, and gloves on when I realized, "I never did that pregnancy test!"

Oops.

I ran upstairs, dipped the stick into the cup ("One one-thousand, two one-thousand . . ."), put the cap back on the stick and began to turn away to resume the off-to-school flurry, when something caught my eye.

There, before my eyes, in only a few seconds (much less time than the suggested two minutes) was a dark blue + sign, as plain as day. I almost fell over as sheer joy and complete and total surprise filled my body. That Universe! Just when you think you have things figured out....

The previous night and the night before that, when I lay in bed tossing and turning, unable to sleep and feeling starving, it didn't occur to me that I could be pregnant. It didn't occur to me that that had been my pattern for my last three pregnancies—I would know I was pregnant because I'd have difficulty falling asleep or wake up in the middle of the night starving, even if I've eaten abundantly during the day and night. It didn't "occur" to me because I had totally let go (surrender—an important aspect of Deliberate Creation).

I had had an epiphany a week and a half earlier on my yoga mat that I was going to begin my "immersion" that very day. My "pregnancy immersion." It was time that I really commit to this "project." After all, "At the moment of commitment, the Universe conspires to assist you."

I'd had so many fun, adventurous projects going on (running our four Prana Power Yoga studios; teaching four doubles a week at the studios; Prana Power Yoga Teacher Training 2009; The Abundant Prana Conference; O Water—my three kids and I were going to have our own label; writing a children's book; creating and teaching The Prana Cleanse™; creating, building, and staffing the Prana Restaurant; writing for Super-mom.com; and, most of all, being a Super-mom to my three children), that I hadn't given "Project Dakota" (as my husband and I had come to affectionately call our intention of having a fourth child) my full-on focus.

"That was going to change. Right now!" I had told myself with a smile that morning on my mat. This was a different sort of resolution than those I'd had in the past. There was no frustration, impatience, anger, regret, guilt, or fear attached to this intention. It was truly and purely a focus, and it felt good.

Here was the "Project Dakota Immersion Plan" that my Spirit laid out for me to insure I got pregnant with my precious little Dakota: meditate on the baby, visualize, say my mantra a lot ("I'm pregnant, I feel great, and I go to sleep at eight"), get acupuncture every other day for fertility, and take Clomid.

"Clomid?" You ask. "Isn't that a Western med and isn't it, uh, a fertility medicine?" You got that straight. And I was on a mission to take it. But that meant finding some—and fast.

I was amazed that my Spirit was advocating medicine because I don't take any medicine except thyroid hormone because I have an anti-thyroid antibody. But I always listen when my higher self speaks, no matter how my mind disagrees with the message. A regular yoga practice is helpful in doing this, in ignoring the mind and listening to the Spirit.

Clomid, for those of you who've never heard of it, is a medicine you can take to help you ovulate, and roughly ten percent of those who take it have twins. That's a loose definition, but that's what we have Google for.

After I explained my "Project Dakota Immersion Plan" to Philippe, we both became ecstatic with the thought of twins. "Two babies with one pregnancy!" we giggled, "What could be better?"

A kick-a** Ob/Gyn in Boston (and a friend of a friend), agreed to hook me up with some Clomid. She asked me to do some blood work and come in and see her before she handed it over. "Ugh, I just want the Clomid," I thought, "Can't she just write me a script?" This is an example of resistance, of not going with the higher flow of the Universe, which don't behoove the process of Deliberate Creation.

A moment later I came back to my breath and the process—the path—of "The Immersion." Many hours on my mat (Practice one) has taught me (and will teach you) to trust the process. To hold your vision. See it. And trust the process. So I turned my boat downstream and let go of the oars.

Many hours on my mat has taught me to trust the process.

I went in for the blood work on a Monday. Our appointment—to get the Clomid—was that Friday morning. I subbed out the two classes that I taught at Prana Power Yoga Newton that Friday morning to make the appointment with the OB, a clear indication to the Universe of my commitment to "The Project" and "The Immersion." The doctor had told me that I'd start taking the Clomid on day five of my period, and that I needed to wean Phoenix, then twenty-six months, immediately.

I weaned Phoenix easily thanks to Philippe who took over his bedtime routine, and breathed a sigh of relief and freedom as I experienced the first time I had not been pregnant and/or nursing in six years.

My energy increased from not nursing and I felt great. I said my mantra all day every day ("I'm pregnant, I feel great, and I go to sleep at eight.") and one night after getting the three kids down I glanced at the clock and realized it was actually possible for me to get to bed somewhere in the eight o'clock range. I was amazed. "It's happening," I thought with a smile. This was Deliberate Creation in action!

But still, no period. Where was it? I was way past day thirty-one (when I'd gotten it the month before) and of course day twenty-seven and twenty-nine (the two months before that), so where was it? My friend Adrienne kept saying, "Maybe you're pregnant." "No, I'm not. I know I'm not," I replied dismissively. "When I had my blood work done for my thyroid last Monday," I continued, "the pregnancy test was negative. And those tests are always accurate."

The second night that I couldn't sleep I crept downstairs to eat raw chocolate pudding (we were still raw vegan at the time) as the clock ticked away a night I would remember for the rest of my life. I thought to myself as I savored one of my favorite raw foods on the planet, "Well, maybe I'll do a pregnancy test tomorrow, just to be sure, and if I am pregnant, I won't tell Philippe, and then when we're supposed to be driving to the doctor appointment tomorrow morning to get the Clomid, I'll give him a big box all wrapped up beautifully with a huge bow, and inside it he'll find the positive pregnancy test stick and I'll say, "Surprise!"

I smiled at the thought and then fell fast asleep, full of raw chocolate pudding and gratitude for the ability to finally catch some zzzzz's. I'm pregnant!

So what do you think I did when that stick said home run? Ran downstairs and into the mudroom where I found Philippe and the kids finishing up the pre-school prep, and blurted out the best news ever, "I'm pregnant!"

So much for the surprise in the big fancy gift box, but this surprise needed no gift-wrap.

# Chapter 19

# The Teacher

"This too shall pass."
- King Solomon

In early April 2009 I had a new and very wise teacher. His name was Dakota Aspen Wells. He was eight weeks old and growing in my belly. And that tiny little being—the size of a grape—had changed my life more in a week than I could ever describe.

Mostly, Dakota had taught me to slow down. This baby gave me no choice—strong Spirit that he was.

I began vomiting eleven times a day, feeling chilled, exhausted, weak, and constantly nauseous. I surrendered, subbed out my classes for a few weeks, and hit the couch.

No food looked, sounded, smelled, or tasted edible, let alone good. I smiled when my friend who, when asked for any suggestions on how to alleviate my symptoms (I would try anything), said, "I never really had that. Maybe eat what sounds good?" She clearly had never had these symptoms because nothing sounded good.

Yet I was so hungry. My stomach growled as I stood in front of the fridge, tears streaming down my face, wishing something—anything—looked somewhat appealing. My food aversions were so strong that I made an official rule in our home: "No baking anything until Mommy feels better! If you want to bake something with your friends, go to our neighbor's." When our then twelve-year-old daughter's friends were over, they loved to bake. And so even though we were raw vegan at the time, this Super-mom didn't stand in their way—unless I was pregnant and the smell of anything baking was repulsive to me. One night my kids baked wheat-free, vegan brownies at a sleepover at our house and I woke up several times in the night to the lingering smell, and had to run for the bathroom.

It's amazing how in a moment your perspective can change. I saw our next-door-neighbors walking down our shared driveway one day coming back from an outing (maybe the park, I thought to myself) and I yearned for "the days" (a week before) when I could run around in the park with my kids. Before I was so exhausted and nauseous that I could barely make it from the couch to the bathroom to throw up.

I was still practicing yoga though because I knew how super-important it was for me to move my energy and keep my Prana flowing. I forced myself onto my mat and took my time. My practice looked very different than it did even a week before, and I found newfound compassion and appreciation for new students who have yet to garner strength in their practice. I was still practicing Deliberation Creation as well. The third Practice just wasn't a-happenin because of the nausea and food aversions, and that's OK. Do what you can with what you have in each moment. It's what you do most of the time that matters.

My kids were actually psyched that Mommy was hanging out on the couch in the playroom watching them play all day. What Super-mom of three sits (ok, lies) on the couch watching her kids' every move? None—unless they're sick with nausea and fatigue. We had a lot of time to play hair salon—one of Phoenix and Sagey's favorite games at the time—which was helpful because as the kids brushed my hair, it kind of distracted me from the discomfort.

I was so grateful to be pregnant with my fourth child and so grateful to be able to watch my other three kids run about—a reminder of why I was going through the symptoms I was experiencing. With my first child, it was more challenging because I didn't have a child in front of me to remind me that it's all worth it. I used to look at a baby gift that I received quite early in my pregnancy, a onesie, and say "OK, Sister, THIS is why you feel this way." But a onesie isn't as powerful as three beautiful, healthy, happy kids running about.

So I reminded myself that "this too shall pass" and utilized Deliberate Creation by ignoring what I didn't want and focusing instead on a text from my friend Dianne who has four kids herself that read, "Hang in there and remember, before you know it, this will be a distant memory."

# Chapter 20

# The Loss

"The only way out is through."
- Robert Frost

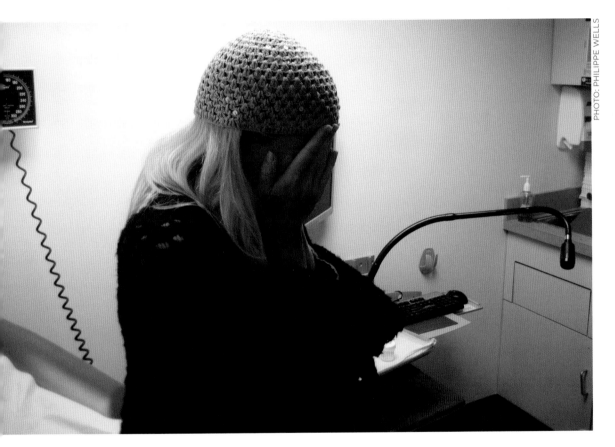

PHOTO: PHILIPPE WELLS

On Tuesday, May 5, 2009 I lost my baby. It was a day I will always remember with indescribable grief and loss.

My baby actually stopped growing at eight weeks and one day—almost three weeks before I began bleeding. But it was at eleven weeks that I learned that I was "no longer pregnant."

Yet I still "felt" pregnant. Still had the nausea, food aversions, vomiting, and the cute belly where my baby once lived and grew happily. I asked my midwife why this was so as we sat in the private office after the ultrasound that changed my life forever—in an instant. "Why then did I throw up eleven times a few nights ago and feel nauseous last night?" I inquired in the state of disbelief, denial, and overall insanity that one faces when told that they have lost a pregnancy. "Your hormones are still in full-force. It's just that the baby is no longer growing and viable," she explained with love and compassion. Harsher words I could not imagine at the time. All the vomiting, nausea, and discomfort—but no baby.

That scene will be forever etched into my memory, as will the half an hour or so I waited to "hear the news" after the ultrasound had ended. It's CYA now ("cover your A**")—a legal thing—that the ultrasound technicians can't say a word to you—not a peep, not a wink that might ease your mind, just a little. Nothin'. Thank the Universe I knew about this policy. My midwife warned me about it before I drove to the hospital.

So I paced the halls waiting for my midwife to come and deliver the news that my Spirit had known for some time, if I were really truthful with myself. I couldn't bring myself to wait in the waiting room with the TV blaring toxic news, the radiation room right next door radiating more toxicity, and a handful of bewildered-looking elderly people sitting gingerly in their chairs, dressed in paper gowns, nervously awaiting their ultrasounds for God only knows what—poor loves. So I paced and I texted. The iPhone is a helpful tool in distraction and denial.

When the midwife found me I followed her into a private room and as she closed the door I turned to her and said, "I lost the baby." "Yes, Taylor, you did," she replied, and we both cried—I louder and more desperately, but she had tears streaming down her face.

She explained to me with love and compassion that the baby measured at eight weeks and one day and just "wasn't meant to be. It's not your fault, Taylor," she assured me. "It's nothing you did or didn't do. It was chromosomal."

My mind immediately began to calculate. Eight weeks and one day...it was the day after I had arrived in Miami after a thirty-eight-hour train ride from Boston. That was the day that my baby's Spirit had chosen to leave my body. I thanked the Universe immediately out loud that I had chosen to take the train instead of a plane (I don't fly during my first trimester due to the radiation), because had I flown, my mind would now be creating a story around how I "caused" my miscarriage by flying—how it was "my fault," etc. Silly, I realize, but the mind likes to create suffering.

As I struggled to start and finish my practice on that day in early May 2009 through fits of sobbing and moments of disbelief ("This must be a nightmare—I am living a nightmare"), I was reminded over and over again of the countless Super-moms who have endured this experience—and some more than once. I met and became friends with a Super-mom in Miami with four beautiful children who had endured twelve miscarriages.

As I had driven to the hospital that morning, heading to get an ultrasound after my intuition and my body told me something was very wrong the night before, I was sobbing while on the cell phone with one of my very best friends who was comforting me, telling me that the baby was fine. I didn't have the heart to tell her that the baby wasn't fine—that I had lost my faith—and the baby. I knew that the baby was gone because even in the very worst of situations as a child growing up in a home that was filled with trauma, I never lost my faith. It was—and is—strong. So to not feel the faith that the baby was fine, told me intuitively that the unspeakable and unthinkable was true—my baby was gone.

As I listened to my friend's sweet words and loving compassion driving to the hospital that morning, I attempted to really take it in. I told her that I was feeling the pain so many women had felt before me on this planet who had miscarried a baby, and I felt connected with them around the issue. "You need to focus on you," she advised. "Let go of all of the others for now and just focus on you."

But my mind kept connecting with all of the Super-moms who have suffered this indescribable loss, many in silence, due to the somewhat antiquated "custom" of waiting three months before announcing one's pregnancy. I personally have never had the discipline to wait to tell (anyone who'll listen) that I'm pregnant, and have always rationalized that if, God forbid, something did happen to the baby, I would want the support of my family and friends. I stood by my rationalization in that moment of utter devastation and grief.

Feeling the energy of so many beautiful people sending me light was of great help and comfort, even if I was not yet in a place to connect with them except via computer. One-on-one conversations just couldn't happen yet—I just ended up sobbing and they couldn't understand a thing I was saying and it was just awkward and painful for us both. So I was grateful for the computer. I could disseminate the painful news through cyberspace and have the personal space that I needed to grieve and eventually heal.

Little by little, pieces of the puzzle began to fall into place. I had never felt the baby's Spirit enter my body with this pregnancy, as I did with all three of my other pregnancies. Several times during the pregnancy a quiet voice whispered, "Something is wrong." I ignored the words, said my mantra about my baby being healthy, happy, and strong, and never told a soul. My breasts never got bigger, as they did immediately with my other three pregnancies. They hurt, but they never got bigger.

My Spirit knew better.

The night I had arrived in Miami by train (I took the train solo while Philippe and our three kids flew) my family picked me up at the station and we stopped at Whole Foods en route to our hotel. I found myself frantically eating pre-packaged raw vegan foods before even paying for them. Frantic doesn't capture the energy with which I was scarfing down raw pesto on crackers, sun seed burgers, and brownies. It was really odd—not my usual energy at all. Then when we arrived at the hotel I ran for the bathroom and threw up twenty-six times.

The following morning (the day my baby's heart stopped beating), I sobbed during my practice inexplicably. My kids asked me what was wrong and I explained that I didn't know. I just couldn't stop crying. Also very unlike me.

The next weekend when I taught at David Wolfe's Superhero Seminar in Maine, I wasn't myself while teaching. I couldn't find my voice, and taught a B- class at best. Teaching usually feels like "home" to me, comes very naturally, and is one of my very favorite things to do along with spending time with my kids and husband and writing. After I taught the class Philippe asked with love, "What happened? What was that? That was so not you. Were you nervous?" to which I replied, "No, I wasn't nervous. Something was off. Something IS off. I just don't feel like myself. I couldn't find my voice and there was nothing I could do to shift it. I felt strangely out of my body. That was so not me and I don't know why. Something is happening, and I don't know what it is. I feel dead inside." Keenly aware of Deliberate Creation, I usually never use the word "dead" to describe anything (a phone losing its charge, etc.) because it has a very low vibration.

I arrived home from Maine that night to a feeling of loss and despair, and cried for hours every day for the entire week, again inexplicably and uncharacteristically. I chalked it up to "re-entry issues," a common experience when one "re-enters" "everyday life" after going on a retreat. But my Spirit knew better.

A week later, as I shared the sad news of losing my baby with loved ones, friends, and family, I was stunned by the number of people who came out of the woodwork and described their similar devastating losses. One of my best friends from Brown texted me the stats, lovingly trying to ease my pain ("One in three pregnancies end in miscarriage"). My midwife corrected her statistic on the phone as we discussed my hormone levels and whether I would need a DNC. "You were a statistical anomaly, Taylor," she explained. "After age thirty-five one out of every two pregnancies ends in a miscarriage, and you had three healthy pregnancies." This made me feel even more compassion for all of the Super-moms going through the same process.

Why doesn't anyone talk about the pain of such a commonly occurring experience? Perhaps precisely because it is so painful. For days I was unable to have a conversation with anyone besides my husband and children, and even those conversations ended with me sobbing.

Another thing I was totally unprepared for was the physical pain. I experienced almost as much physical pain losing my baby as I did with my three labors with my three children. The cramping, bleeding, clotting, and pain in my back, thighs, and gluts was unbearable at times. I took 600 mg of Advil to ease it, which did no good. My midwife gave me Percocet and I tucked it away in the medicine cabinet, just in case. The unbelievably intense pain of the contractions of labor and of pushing a full-term baby out during labor is more intense; however, the pain during my miscarriage was relentless and continuous.

So a big shout out to all of you Super-moms who've endured this, some of you in silence. You rock my world, and you, in fact, created and continue to create our world. For without you being the Super-mom that you are and bringing your beautiful child(ren) into this world despite the (pretty high) chance that your pregnancy could have ended with this type of devastating loss (this never entered my mind with my other children or this child...I now understand that I was beyond naïve), the world as we know it would not exist.

A big shout out to you for creating the beautiful child(ren) you have, despite the nausea, the vomiting, the food aversions, the fear, the fatigue, the varicose veins, the weight gain, the backaches, the heartburn, the cravings, the headaches, the tender breasts, the hormonal emotional rollercoaster, the discomfort, the extremely difficult emotions that can surface after delivery (post-partum depression), and more.

I have the utmost respect for your courage and strength to pull through after losing a baby to miscarriage if you have...to sob, grieve, let go, and eventually carry on. To still pack the lunches for school, read the bedtime story, and get the glasses of water at bedtime for your child(ren) as your "hospital style" double maxi pad needs to be changed yet again before it ruins another pair of PJ's. But you soldier on, Super-mom.

And this is just one of the many reasons you have earned the name: SUPER-MOM.

How do you utilize the three Practices of creating the best life ever when you are suffering from a devastating loss like miscarriage? You do your best, with breath. You draw upon the strength you've cultivated in your life thus far and you ask for help—from your friends, your family, and the Universe. Your yoga practice is incredibly helpful, as it was to me during this trying time. Deliberate Creation is also helpful. Attempting to distract yourself as often as possible from the negative thoughts that accompany grief will bring some much-needed relief and buy some time, which is what you need to heal. And the eating? Well you most likely care very little about food during this time, which makes it a good time to practice eating what you love in moderation. Give yourself the comfort of the foods you love (even if you don't feel like eating a thing) and it will be easy for you to eat just the right amount of them because let's face it, food is the last thing on your mind. This will in turn help you to set the template for allowing yourself any foods you want and love in moderation, without the panicked overeating that sometimes accompanies the consumption of foods we love, because somewhere sometime in our lives we've been told we can't or shouldn't have them.

It's a beginning again of sorts. Very healing, very cleansing, and very in line with creating the best life ever.

# Chapter 21

# The Lesson

*"Faith is the bird that sings when the dawn is still dark."*
*- Rabindranath Tagore*

Fifty-four hours after I lost my baby on Tuesday, May 5, 2009, I was amazed at the change possible in such a small period of time. I only had to stop once during my yoga practice to cry. I was able to accept that it did indeed happen and it was not some sort of bizarre extended nightmare. I was able to find gratitude for many things: my three healthy, wonderful, sparkly, happy children; my soul mate who had been with me every step of the way through the harrowing process and with whom I was even closer due to the painful path; my yoga practice which always brings me a sense of relief both physically and emotionally when all else seems confusing and painful at best; my incredible family, friends, and community who were amazingly supportive, loving, kind, and compassionate, even though I couldn't speak live to anyone yet since any conversation ended with me sobbing and no one really understanding what I was saying; the sun which came out the day before to let me know that one day I would find, feel, and live in the light again (it poured rain the whole day I found out my baby was gone); the internet for allowing me to disseminate the painful news through cyberspace and have the personal space I needed to grieve and heal; the grass that was getting greener with each passing day; the smiles on my children's faces; my son's expression the night before while I was reading him a bedtime story and he began pounding on my stomach and looked at me for a reaction, and I said, "That's OK, you can do that now because the baby is gone. The baby is in Heaven," and he looked up to the sky with the expression of an angel and said "Baby Kota;" the raw nut milk that my eleven-year-old brought me to say, "I hope you're feeling better, Mom;" the many friends who came through for me by helping me find someone to perform a DNC asap when my midwife practice couldn't fit me in for awhile, and the angel on earth who ultimately performed it for me that day in her office and without anesthesia (the same Ob/Gyn who was lined up to hook me up with Clomid); my yoga studios and all of our students, who are a constant source of light in my life; and the baby who brought so much light, love, and joy to my life for almost eleven weeks, and whose Spirit will always be with my family and me, watching over us and bringing us wisdom and love.

I didn't yet have the lesson for my painful experience, but I knew that it would come, with time and healing. As a friend wrote to me that day, "Time will heal, and reveal."

So whatever you're going through right now, hang in there and breathe. One moment at a time. Do your best to get on your yoga mat when you can muster the strength, search for the best thought possible in this moment without slipping into denial (Deliberate Creation is not about denial) and allow yourself total freedom with your eating. In time you will have found peace, relief, wisdom, and ultimately, gratitude for all of the aforementioned. No matter how impossible that seems right now.

# Chapter 22

# The Wake Up Call

The key to getting in the Vortex
is to be in a state of appreciation.

PHOTO: KELLY LORENZ

After I lost my baby I was waiting for the lesson. Why had my Spirit attracted the awful and dark experience into my aura? It had been three days since the ultrasound and I asked myself over and over again, "What's the lesson? What do I need to learn? What do I need to do differently?"

Then it came—just like that. The wake up call.

I thought I lived gratitude. I thought I lived grace. I thought I walked and lived in the light, and helped teach this to others. But losing a baby I never got to hold moved me way up the scale in the gratitude department. It was the wake up call. And I heard it, loud and clear.

Helping my kids brush their teeth and put on their PJ's, making them breakfast, packing their lunches, picking them up from school or yoga class, and yes, even doing their laundry would never be the same again. These activities that were formerly taken for granted, or, at times when

I was a super-tired Super-mom, even somewhat annoying, were now being experienced almost as though I was in slow motion. I was really and truly enjoying every moment.

I was talking with my friend about this when she picked up her daughter from a play date at our home. She too had experienced a miscarriage and when I told her how I was so appreciative and grateful now for my kids, like over-the-top grateful when I even just looked at them in a way that had never even possible before, she said, "Yes! Exactly! Losing my baby had the same effect on me!"

**I am grateful for this wisdom.**

So...gratitude. The wake up call. I get it. Point taken.

"But was it really necessary?" I asked myself repeatedly. "Why couldn't I have done some more asana and meditation to become even more grateful and present? And had my baby be healthy, happy, and strong, like my mantra said?"

I didn't have that answer yet but I knew it was coming. I felt it. Looking for the lesson in every experience on your path is an important part of Deliberate Creation. Ask the Universe for the lesson and open your heart and the lesson will become clear when you're ready. The more yoga you practice and the more freedom you truly live (Practices two and three), the quicker and easier this process will become.

My baby's Spirit came in to teach me a lesson, and then went on his or her way back into the light after eight weeks and one day. I was grateful for the wisdom I was given and will carry it with me always. As I will carry my baby's Spirit with me in my heart.

# Chapter 23

# The Shift

Wake up and smell the nag champa.

PHOTO: PHILIPPE WELLS

Five days after I lost my baby I had an enormous shift, for which I was incredibly grateful.

After the worst Mother's Day ever, I was putting Sagey (then age five) to bed and she said, "I remember the day that you found out that you were 'pregnant.' You came running downstairs and we were all in the mudroom and you said, 'I'm 'pregnant!' I'm 'pregnant!' I'm 'pregnant!'"

"That was a happy day," I replied.

"Now all the days are sad," Sagey said quietly.

"Dear God," I thought, "I didn't think I could feel any worse, but now I do."

I was feeling almost as bad about the meltdowns I'd been having out of "nowhere" since losing my baby as I did about my immense loss (*almost* is a key word here).

I was not at all myself, which is of course OK or even expected when you are grieving, but what came to me via my Spirit in that moment was:

"WAKE UP! THIS IS IT! THIS IS THE ONLY MOMENT THAT MATTERS. THIS IS ALL YOU'VE GOT. WAKE UP! COME BACK! REMEMBER WHO YOU ARE. DO I WANT TO BE PRESENT AND A SUPER-MOM TO MY THREE AMAZING KIDS WHO ARE HERE IN MY LIFE AND LIVING IN THE NOW, OR BE IN THE PAST AND NOT BE PRESENT FOR THEM BECAUSE I AM SO INCREDIBLY SAD, ANGRY, CONFUSED, DEVASTATED, EMPTY, CONFUSED, ETC. ABOUT MY BABY WHO IS GONE? DO I WANT TO BE THE BEST I CAN BE IN THIS MOMENT FOR ALL LIVING BEINGS AND LIVE PEACE, LOVE, AND JOY, WHILE HONORING THE PAST AND ACKNOWLEDGING IT, OR LIVE IN THE PAST, IN ANGER AND DESPAIR AND FEAR? DO I WANT TO SHOW MY KIDS IT'S OK OR EVEN GOOD TO CRY BUT ALSO THAT IT'S IMPORTANT TO STAY PRESENT AND GROUNDED AND HAVE GRATITUDE FOR WHAT IS?"

Then I couldn't sleep, as had been the pattern since I lost the baby, even though I was so incredibly exhausted. And for the first time since my loss, I sat and meditated.

What I felt was a miracle. Such an incredible outpouring of love and light filling my body through my heart, my seventh chakra, and my open palms. I was actually embodying the love and light that so many beautiful souls had been sending me. I felt it and I embodied it. Then I fell asleep.

I woke up to my alarm after very little sleep and although my head ached from sleep deprivation and all that my physical body had been enduring for the days since I lost the baby, I sprang out of bed in a similar fashion to Scrooge after his life-changing night. I went to the kitchen, made my kids raw vegan breakfast in bed, and then woke them up with joy.

"Mommy's back!" I cheered, and they all beamed and squealed with delight at the sight of raw chocolate chip cookies shaped into hearts, raw heart chocolates, raw vanilla macaroons, apple slices, pear slices, raw chocolate pudding, and vanilla nut milk. They didn't skip a beat and began chatting about the day to come and how beautiful the sun was in the sky.

After dropping my kids at school and receiving countless hugs and tearful, "I'm sorry's," I went to Prana Power Yoga Newton and practiced with my husband. My body was surprisingly strong after the whole ordeal, and I soaked up the practice like a sponge and didn't cry once—a different experience than the other two times I'd practiced at Prana Newton since I'd lost the baby when I sobbed several times during the practice.

I booked out of the studio right after class before anyone could inquire how I was feeling (most didn't know I'd lost the baby and would end up feeling awful and embarrassed if they asked, so I was hoping they could read it on Super-mom.com before connecting with me live to avoid the awkwardness) and went home to shower and eat from the abundant refrigerator in our kitchen, thanks to so many wonderful friends and students who had bestowed lots of delicious food upon us since we'd lost the baby.

That night as I went to sleep I was in awe of the resiliency of the human spirit. I was in no way in denial and was very aware of what I had lost, but was also keenly aware of what I had gained, utilizing Deliberate Creation. What had I gained? Even more gratitude and presence in the NOW than ever before. Even more connection with other beings. A lot of compassion and empathy for every Super-mom who has gone through this type of loss or other losses and every Super-person who's been through any type of loss. Even more joy in each moment, when possible, and when not, even more surrender to what is. "What is" may be sobbing or being quiet or wanting to be left alone, and that's OK. A total surrender to the flow of life and a real understanding that time and control are illusions. A commitment to taking it one day at a time and just seeing what tomorrow brings. And a deep understanding that I was in the midst of creating the best life ever. I'd learned on an even deeper level from my loss that I was already living it. And that I was in the process (as are you) of creating even more love, more joy, and more peace, with my daily yoga practice, Deliberate Creation, and consuming the foods I love with no restriction. I was still raw vegan at the time and believed that I was totally free in my relationship with food, but later I would learn that an even bigger sense of freedom was possible in this area. The truly remarkable thing about creating the best life ever is that our minds cannot even conceive of how good it can and will get if we regularly utilize the three Practices and allow. When I was raw vegan for seven years I felt so free in my eating because I ate "anything and everything that I want and as much as I want whenever I want—all raw vegan food," which was a huge improvement from how I'd eaten for many years of my life, restricting this or that, as most people do. But I was to learn that even more joy and freedom was possible in this area. The Universe has plans for you that you don't even know about. Utilizing the three Practices will line you up with these magnificent and divine plans. And it's fun while you do it. It's a never-ending process of joy. And that's what it's all about, isn't it? Joy.

# Chapter 24

# The Projection

*"Whatever happens around you, don't take it personally.*
*Nothing other people do is because of you.*
*It is because of themselves."*
*- Don Miguel Ruiz*

PHOTO: KELLY LORENZ

One thing that I never would've expected, along with losing my baby, were the responses I got from people after my loss. The outpouring of support and love I received was beyond incredible. The gratitude I felt for this support beyond words.

Another energetic response from many people was also unanticipated and quite interesting, indeed. I noticed that the loss of my baby brought me "closer" in several ways (some energetic, some more visible) with many people—people with whom I was already very close, friends, people whom before were just acquaintances, students, and fellow Super-moms.

Philippe and I were talking about this phenomenon, because he had noticed it too. "It's as though people can relate to you now. It's like before they thought you were 'perfect' and had never experienced anything difficult in your life," Philippe said at a soccer game after yet another Super-mom connected with me deeply around my loss, a Super-mom with whom I had attempted to connect countless times at our kids' activities but had always been met with an unequivocal "no dice."

After he said the words, we both started laughing at the thought of my never having experienced anything difficult. The funny thing about grief is that grief and humor are intricately connected. If you've ever grieved, you know exactly what I'm talking about. It wasn't uncommon for me to be sobbing one minute and laughing a few minutes later. It's a healthy—albeit odd—way to shift and move energy.

The reason Philippe and I laughed is that I have actually endured even more than my "fair share" of grief and loss in this lifetime. I'm OK with it all now and have healed my heart from the heartbreak endured in my childhood and in my twenties when I chose to deal with the childhood I really had instead of the one I'd made up in my mind to get through it all. I have found forgiveness for all involved and am grateful for what I went through, since it made me the person I am today. My past pain and suffering makes me able to connect, understand, empathize, and just "get" where pretty much any student I teach is coming from. So deep, varied, and far-reaching were my experiences of loss that I can quite literally "feel" the pain of many. And they can feel this—they know intuitively that I feel it, even if they can't quite put their finger on it.

I never teach from my mind—I teach from my heart and my Spirit. Two things that for many years were broken but now shine brightly, proving that complete and total healing is possible for anyone. The three Practices of creating the best life ever were essential in my healing. I utilized all three of them daily.

"Why are you being so vague about what you actually went through?" you ask, curious about what I could have possibly experienced and still walk around saying daily, "Have the best day ever." The answer is that it doesn't matter. The details don't matter at this point and in fact, I made a choice many years ago to let the details—my "story"—go. More specifically, to let the darkness go and focus on the light. I had a choice. I made it, and I never looked back. This is the essence of Deliberate Creation. Deliberately Creating means deliberately choosing on what to focus. How does it feel to talk about this? How does it feel to think about this? How does it feel to write about this? Deliberately choosing what to talk, think, and write about, and thereby, utilizing the Law of Attraction to create the best life ever.

For years, I bravely told my story—my truth about what happened to me as a child— to all of those people in my life who mattered to me. I let go of the initial shame that accompanied my trauma history and found the courage to speak my truth and, ultimately, to heal. All of my relationships—except two—grew stronger.

I was going to write a book to "tell the world" what happened to me and ostensibly help the many out there who have also endured trauma(s). But then one day I had clarity. To really help—to really heal myself and help others to heal themselves (I believe that we all heal ourselves, that "healers" are only "helpers" in this process), meant for me to walk toward and in the light. To spread the light. To teach the light. I survived my pain and soldiered on by remembering who I was and being the light that I was and am and that you are. And I chose to teach others how to do the same. This was a big crossroads in my life.

So many years later, as I endured the pain and heartbreak of losing my baby, it was interesting to notice that somehow, through my teachings of finding the light and following it even in the worst of circumstances, I had come to be the source of a great deal of projection. I suppose that people had made me what they need or needed me to be. Perhaps they looked at my joy and the light that I live and assumed it was always this way with and for me, that I was born into the best home ever and "had it made" from day one.

Things are not always what they seem. In fact, one thing I've learned from my pain is that most often, things are not what they seem.

But now I do live in the light and radiate that light. Because I have chosen to do so. This is Deliberate Creation. Cultivating and utilizing your yoga practice and freedom in eating help in this process. They are tools that help you to create deliberately. To create your best life ever.

So today as you walk your path, be mindful. Tuck this awareness in your heart and notice if you find yourself projecting something onto another who may have a story you know nothing about. The biggest gift you can give them—and anyone—is not just your open heart, but your open mind as well.

# Chapter 25

# I Will Feel Whole and Complete When...

## Stop waiting to live. This is IT.
## This is the only moment that matters.

On August 1, 2009 I got my period right as I was leaving to teach yoga at David Wolfe's Superhero Seminar in New Hampshire. Kids in the car, engine running, I ran into the house to go potty quickly before we took off and bam! There it was. I was bummed.

We'd been trying to get pregnant again since I'd lost our baby a few months before, and that month I was sure I was pregnant.

Thanks to my yoga and Deliberate Creation practices, I let it go pretty quickly, moved on, and had a lot of clarity from the Universe about needing to really let go, live my life, and stop "waiting."

Since I'd lost the baby, I wasn't doing some things that I'd wanted to do because "I might be pregnant" or because we were trying. I wasn't waking up at four am to write, work, and practice before my kids wake up, which I love to do because I love the quiet of that time of day. I wasn't doing a juice fast to detox after my loss. I wasn't doing some cool new intense yoga poses I wanted to try on my mat. I wasn't putting DMSO on my bone spurs, and so on. I was also forcing myself to eat heavier raw vegan foods late at night (we were still raw vegan at the time) so that I wouldn't get too skinny because some say it's better to have more meat on your bones to get pregnant. After I ate heavy foods late, I would have bizarre nightmares and wake up in the morning hung over because my body doesn't like eating heavy foods late at night, preferring lighter foods so I can sleep well and wake up clear, energized, and happy.

But I wasn't pregnant yet and I took a deep breath in and a deep breath out and said to myself, "I will be pregnant at the perfect time, and for now, I'm movin' on and livin.'" This is the letting go essential for Deliberate Creation. This is the mandatory surrendering to the process.

Not that I wasn't living before. I still had a bunch of great things going on in my life, abundance, and "distractions" from thinking about getting pregnant and, of course, my three wonderful children and husband to love and cherish. But it was energetic, and that Friday night when I got my period, it became clear.

After we'd lost the baby, I kept saying to Philippe, "I know we're not 'done.' I know Dakota is coming. I see us with four kids...or, actually, five. I think Dakota is coming back with his brother, Montana. I think that's why he left us after 8 weeks, because Montana didn't make it into the earth plane the first go-around. I feel both of the baby's Spirits in my aura. And I will feel whole and complete when they are here. My twin sons. Then I can relax and just enjoy them all, all five of them, and live." Philippe said that he was rooting for twins (they run in my family), totally saw the babies too, and knew we'd have five kids one day. At the perfect time.

Then I realized that me saying, "I will feel whole and complete when Dakota and Montana come," is no different than someone saying, "I will feel whole and complete when I meet the right guy, graduate from school, buy the best house ever, have the best job ever, make a million dollars, lose ten pounds, etc." It's putting life on hold until...(fill in the blank), and then I'll feel complete. I'm very happy and very grateful most of the time and have the best day ever every day, so this energy was subtle, yet palpable.

Then the wisdom came: "I am whole and complete NOW. In this moment. I feel this in my body, mind, and Spirit. I feel the essence of this and live it daily."

And I wasn't saying and feeling the essence of this just so the babies would come faster (Deliberate Creation says you must find the essence of what you want and feel it before it will happen). I really felt it and was living it moment to moment. So that's what the babies coming to us one day had taught me already. Wise teachers.

I also chose to not talk about trying to get pregnant with people anymore. And this Super-mom needed discipline for that because it was so fun for me to talk about and so sisterly. But I was re-reading "Miracles" by Stuart Wilde and realized that one of the steps of manifesting is, "Don't talk about your miracle with anyone. This drastically dissipates the energy of the manifestation." So true. I totally know this and teach it all the time, but somehow I was forgetting it regarding getting pregnant. I had stepped off the path. So I stepped back on. Ready to continue to create my best life ever with the three Practices that had worked and continued to work so well for me.

What are you putting your life on hold for?

# Chapter 26

# The Gift

"Follow your bliss and the Universe will open
doors for you where there were only walls."
- Joseph Campbell

On Wednesday September 4, 2009, on our new Prana Restaurant's opening day, in the oh-so-wee hours of the morning, I did a pregnancy test.

We'd been "trying;" however, that month had been different. I had truly and totally surrendered any attachment to when our babies came and had really not been thinking about it or talking about it at all after my epiphany about being whole and complete in this moment. Right now. Not sometime in the future.

In the darkness of the room, I peered at what appeared to be a line—faint—but nevertheless, a line. "It can't be," I thought to myself way too calmly and in a somewhat disconnected way. "This feels 'too easy.' And the line is so faint." Yet, concurrently, my friend Deb's words echoed through my mind, disagreeing with my logic, "A line's a line!"

I put the stick down and got on my mat, vision blurred from only four hours of sleep after we did everything humanly possible the night before to prepare for our Prana Restaurant's opening day. I purposefully didn't pull a "total all-nighter" since we'd been trying.

After my practice, I grabbed the stick and woke up Philippe. He concurred that the line was pretty faint but there, and I tucked it in my bag for safekeeping. I walked around all day with that pregnancy stick in my bag, peeking at it in moments when no one was looking, utilizing Deliberate Creation. I was getting great joy outta lookin at that stick, and that joy in turn magnetized to me more joy, in many forms.

That night a friend of mine who's psychic called and asked if I was pregnant. I told her about the "faint line" and she laughed out loud. "There's no such thing as a false positive, Taylor! You're pregnant!" I was guarded about feeling the joy, the elation that comes with knowing you are going to have a baby, or two. "You will feel different this time," she explained kindly. She had had miscarriages before she conceived her daughter and son and knew the drill. I was clearly not letting myself get excited, or feel. Anything.

The next morning I tested again and yes, the line was there—oh yes it was there—and so much darker this time. I allowed the joy—the elation—to enter my body, mind, and Spirit. It was as if an enormous light filled my body. More energy and joy than I could ever describe in words.

Again, I woke Philippe in the wee hours, holding the stick one inch from his sleepy eyes. But this time I had tears in my eyes and was shaking—with joy. "Ohhh, Super-mom," he said with love and compassion, and gave me a hug to calm my tears. He thought I was crying because the test was negative. "No!" I exclaimed. "Look! Look! Look at the line! It's there. It's there!" He examined it and saw that yes, it WAS there, and we both squealed with joy.

That day, all day, I told my big news to anyone with whom I came into contact with whom I am close. Now, I love people and feel close to quite a few and I was in and about our Newton Prana Power Yoga Studio and The Prana Restaurant all day...so Sister was spreading the word. I couldn't contain myself! The energy was so strong and amazing.

That night, my psychic friend called me again. "T, I had a hit that you shouldn't tell everyone about your pregnancy. Keep the energy for baby and you." "Oops. Too late!" I said, giggling. "Did you blog about it?" she asked, slightly horrified. "No...but I told about ten people—anyone I love with whom I came into contact today." I told her that I didn't want to come from fear. "See if you can hold the energy, T," she said calmly.

And hold the energy I did. From that moment on that energy surged through my body like no energy I'd ever experienced, and helped my twin pregnancy to be the best pregnancy ever. The day I found out I was pregnant and was telling people, I threw up eleven times. After I stopped spreading the word and holding the energy for the babies and me, I didn't throw up again. I knew I was pregnant with twins because the pregnancy test was positive so early in my cycle, indicating an inordinate amount of HCG. It was confirmed by an ultrasound a week later.

I revamped my "eating strategy" for this pregnancy at the same time that I stopped telling people, so I'm sure both were helpful and instrumental in the shift. I ate little amounts at least every thirty minutes (sometimes every ten minutes if the nausea hit) and chewed my food really well. Eating every ten to thirty minutes is easy, but eating small amounts and chewing well is not—for me, anyway. Especially when I'm pregnant. But it worked, and I kept everything down.

Our babies' ETA was May 7, 2010, one year and one day after I had "lost" Dakota the first go-around. I continued to have the best pregnancy ever, complete with a daily afternoon nap with Phoenix, age two at the time (twins means exhaustion times two), and I am convinced that "holding the energy" while utilizing the three Practices for creating the best life ever manifested my amazing pregnancy with twins at age forty-four. I practiced yoga and Deliberate Creation every single day of my pregnancy and ate everything I loved in moderation. The doctors and midwives marveled at how my pregnancy flowed so easily and well when their other Super-moms pregnant with twins were mostly on bed rest. I practiced yoga and swam a half-mile daily till the day I delivered.

Think about it! If energy, visualization, yoga, and freedom are that powerful, imagine what you can do when you utilize the three Practices regularly. Really imagine, right now, because that's how you create. Your imagination is key; it's the coming attractions of your life. Your best life ever.

# Chapter 27

# The Best Labor and Delivery Ever

*"All good is coming from this situation."*
*- Abraham-Hicks*

On Wednesday April 7, 2010, at just about thirty-six weeks pregnant with my twin boys, I got ready to go to the hospital for a routine weekly midwife checkup and ultrasound. When you're forty-four and pregnant with twins, they do ultrasounds often in the final weeks of pregnancy to make sure that your twins are continuing to thrive. They mostly wanna make sure that one isn't eating more of the food.

Although I'm all about doing things as naturally as possible, I have always had the attitude of "whatever works so my babies are delivered healthfully, happily, and safely. Whatever it takes. No attachment to the 'how,'" which is an important piece of utilizing Deliberate Creation. Let go of the "how" and what it will "look like." Be open to however the Universe delivers your miracle, and it will be delivered quickly, provided you aren't resisting.

As I gathered my stuff together for the checkup, I intuitively knew to have our (then) three and six year-olds hang out at our friend's house while we went in to the hospital. They'd been accompanying us to our hospital visits to learn about hospitals, ultrasounds, eastern and western medicine, doctors, midwives, nurses, etc—homeschooling at it's best! We were homeschooling them at the time while our then twelve year-old was in public middle school. She joined us for a few of the ultrasounds when her schedule allowed.

I texted our friend about my kids coming over for a play date, spontaneously grabbed my overnight hospital suitcase, threw it into the back of our minivan, and scooted to the appointment.

"Hmmmmmm," I thought to myself. "I wonder if my guys are coming today."

At the ultrasound, the babies looked perfect. The doctor said calmly, "They look great and there's no need for alarm, but I'd like to induce you this Friday morning. You are officially thirty-six weeks on Friday—full term for twins—and I'd like them to be born then because baby A is now 4 pounds 12 ounces and baby B is 5 pounds 14 ounces, and I think that they'll do even better out of the womb, nursing and getting equal nutrition from you. It seems that baby B is eating more of the food."

"Great!" I squealed in delight. "Let's have them now! Why wait? I have my overnight bag with me, my kids are at my friend's house playing, and I love the number seven!"

My intuition said it was time. I had no ambivalence and no confusion, just total and complete clarity. A lot of yoga will help you to have clarity in moments like this, and more. Plus I'd been deliberately creating the best labor and delivery ever, so I was confident.

The doctor smiled and said he'd like my midwife to check my cervix dilation and then he'd like me to do a non-stress test in labor and delivery to monitor the babies' heart rates for fifteen minutes and make sure they were doing great, and then we'd talk again. My midwife checked my cervix—three centimeters dilated—and the non-stress test technician confirmed that the twins were doing great.

Philippe and I talked with the nurse in labor and delivery about the possibility of inducing me that day. She said it would be fine; however, the hospital was "full" for the following day with scheduled labor and deliveries. So Friday morning would be better logistically. She also said that the doctor wanted to wait until I was "officially" 36 weeks. "We're talking 30 hours difference, Sister!" I laughed, "That's ridiculous." She agreed that it was silly; but nevertheless, it was "protocol." A believer in paddling downstream and focusing on what I do want (Deliberate Creation) I smiled, let go, and we booked my induction for Friday morning April 9, 2010. They wanted me to come in at 8 am on Friday to be induced, I suggested noon, and we settled on 10 am. "Super-mom needs her sleep before labor, and I need to do my yoga and Deliberate Creation practices so I can be calm, focused, and grounded," I explained.

We drove home elated. We'd be meeting our sons within a day or so! And it all felt right. It felt right because our sons' health and safety was our first concern, not the how's, what's, and details of labor and delivery. Yes, I am a Yogi. Yes, I am a Yoga Instructor. Yes, I am a Spiritual Teacher. Yes, I was raw vegan at the time. Yes, I don't take drugs. Yes, I believe my body can heal itself. Yes, I love natural medicine, eastern medicine, acupuncture, and many alternative healing modalities. And yes, I would do whatever my midwives and doctors recommended for the safe and healthy delivery of my baby boys. As long as my intuition agreed. Unless it was something that felt off and ridiculous and out of balance, like getting to the hospital at 8 am and losing much needed sleep before labor. So I did push against the scheduling piece briefly, and we found a happy compromise.

Once we got home I began to walk our neighborhood. For the first time ever! We'd moved into our new home on November 25, 2009 (the White Castle I talked about in Chapter 9) and I hadn't walked in our neighborhood yet because I'd wanted to keep my babies in utero full-term. We live on a serious hill overlooking Newton, Massachusetts and walking hills can bring on labor. But now I was focused on going into labor naturally if possible since that would be best for my twins, for them to come out sooner rather than later, and why not bring it on naturally if possible?

I walked, or rather waddled, through our neighborhood and neighbors smiled as they watched me pass. What a sight I must have been! My belly was ginormous.

I felt the contractions coming on and getting stronger, and I continued to walk. Then I went home, made my kids the best raw vegan dinner ever, and we all went out to walk again. My contractions continued to come and increase in intensity and frequency. A more exciting time I cannot recall. Time seemed to stand still.

I put my three and six year-olds to bed, finished up a few things for Prana Power Yoga and Prana Restaurant (which we still owned at the time), tied up other loose ends for my consulting practice, cleaned out my email in-box, and then stopped and noticed—everything seemed to be "done" and "in place." There was a sense of calm that pervaded my home, my office, and my entire being.

"They are coming," I smiled. "And I'm ready."

At midnight Philippe and I called my sister in Santa Fe and talked for almost two hours. I hung up with her at 2 am, fell asleep, and awoke at 3:30 am in labor.

I woke Philippe with the classic words "It's time!" and called my dear friend and neighbor, Dianne, who came over within minutes to stay with my kids as we began the journey to meet our baby sons.

We met my doula at the hospital, moved into our beautiful hospital room overlooking the Charles River, and settled in for the best labor and delivery ever. My midwife came in and exclaimed happily, "Oh my God! I remember you! I was there with you last May when you lost your baby. I was there at the ultrasound, remember?"

I was amazed at the synchronicity. Remember, when you utilize the three Practices of creating the best life ever, synchronicities abound. I smiled and said, "Of course you were...and now you're going to deliver my beautiful baby boys and it will all have come full circle. Last May I told you that my baby Dakota wasn't gone, that he was coming back with his brother, Montana. And now he is. It's all perfect."

My midwife smiled, said that she'd gotten the chills when I had said what I said, and that it was one of the most amazing and Spiritual things she'd ever heard in her thirty years as a midwife. She did an ultrasound and I heard her say quietly to one of the nurses "Hmmmmm, baby B is in an interesting position."

I continued to focus on my contractions, which weren't debilitating yet, and practiced Deliberate Creation—deliberately ignoring my midwife's comment about baby B because it freaked me out a little. I chose to focus instead on visualizing and feeling the essence of the best labor and delivery ever. Remember, Deliberate Creation is all about the power of the focus of your mind.

My midwife came back a while later and announced that baby B was now breach and so we'd need to do a C-Section. She explained that none of the doctors at the hospital were comfortable delivering one twin breach, that they'd "been burned" or "had bad experiences" trying to do so.

Wow. Baby B had been head down the afternoon before at my routine ultrasound appointment. Both babies had been head down. So baby B had done a 180-degree flip in the middle of the night. That's why I'd felt nauseous.

"Rock on! Let's do it!" I squealed in delight without skipping a beat. My first and only concern was my babies being delivered safely and healthfully. I was not attached to the "how."

My doula was on a totally different frequency, however, and asked my midwife if she could find a doctor who would do a vaginal delivery with one twin breach. I stopped her mid-sentence and said, "Much gratitude Sister for advocating for Super-mom; however, are you out of your mind? I believe in paddling downstream and if the doctors aren't comfortable for the reasons mentioned, why would we question that? My babies' safety is the first priority. Period." My doula got it, apologized, and we proceeded down the path of least resistance and most safety.

My midwife went to talk with the doctors again and came back with another report—"They would like you to go home and come back tomorrow morning for a scheduled C section—at the same time you were scheduled to be induced." I burst into tears and said firmly, "I'm not going home. Are they out of their minds? I'm in labor for God's sake and I have three children at home who are now in the care of my good friend and they want me to go home IN LABOR, take care of my three kids and then leave again on a moment's notice while in hard labor? Do you know how that will mess with my three kids' minds? And they want me to let my labor get to the point of excruciating, and then do a C? Nope. I won't do it. I'm not going home Sister."

My midwife got it. She left the room again without a word to advocate for me.

At that point, Philippe turned to me and said, "Super-mom, there's no way the doctors are going to agree to do it today. They have their 'schedule' and they're stickin' to it. It's 'protocol' and it's 'CYA' (Cover You're A**)."

But I had hope.

"There's still a chance that they'll do it today. I'm going visualize," I responded. Then I closed my eyes and visualized, practicing Deliberate Creation by focusing on what I wanted, instead of what I didn't want.

My midwife walked in again—no idea how much later—time was oddly irrelevant at this point, and said with a huge smile, "Blast off!" I squealed in delight.

My midwife then said, smiling, "You are totally clear about this. You have no ambivalence." "Yes!" I exclaimed. "Let's do it!"

"Have you eaten anything?" she asked. "Nope," I answered quickly, noting how hungry I was since I'd forgotten to bring anything to eat to the hospital. "Taylor, you had a bite of my apple," my doula reminded me. "Oh, OK, then," my midwife continued, "we'll need to wait eight hours till surgery. It's an anesthesia safety thing." "Great! I'll sleep!" I said, praying I wouldn't go into hard labor during that eight hour time period.

Fast forward to 3:15 pm. The anesthesiologist came in and spent thirty minutes explaining the entire procedure to me so I'd know what to expect. I had had no fear until he started explaining everything to me. Then I felt nervous.

Utilizing Ujayii breath, visualization, meditation, and anything else I could pull outta my sleeve, I stayed calm as they prepped Philippe, my doula, and me for surgery. And in we went.

Talk about surreal. I don't even watch TV, but this was reminiscent of shows I'd watched back in the day ("ER"); however; this time it was me being operated on.

The spinal was a joke. I said to the OR team, "What? That's it? That hurt less than when the nurse takes my blood to check my thyroid levels every six weeks!" Everyone laughed, but there was still a sense of seriousness in that OR that was palpable.

The other two things that were supposed to be "difficult" or "weird" during the C-section were a feeling of not being able to breathe and a feeling of "pressure" on my abdomen. The breathing thing was accurate, but I just inhaled and exhaled calmly and told myself that it was an illusion (it was) and that I was breathing fine. It was more of a "tightness" at the very top of my throat.

The "pressure" description was inaccurate. More accurately, it felt like what it was—people sticking their hands into my body. No pain, but a weird and uncomfortable sensation.

Easier that an all-natural vaginal birth? Absolutely! Easier than a vaginal birth with an epidural? You bet! It was the best ever!

When I heard my first-born twin son Dakota's cry, tears of joy streamed down my face immediately. As they showed me my precious son, I was in heaven. Never mind the fact that my abdomen was still cut open. Dakota Aspen Wells was born. Safely and healthfully.

Next came Montana. Exactly four minutes later. There was a pause—I didn't hear him cry immediately—and as the anesthesiologist kept asking me how I felt (he would do so every fifteen seconds during the surgery to adjust the medicine accordingly) I ignored him and asked repeatedly, "Is my baby OK? Why isn't he crying? Is Montana OK?"

It seemed like a long time but was actually only a matter of seconds, and soon he was crying like his brother. They'd just had to suction out some fluid. Very standard. Montana Sky Wells was born. Safely and healthfully.

I was relieved and elated beyond belief. Joy pervaded every cell of my body, mind, and Spirit. My sons were born, healthy and perfect—weighing in, ironically, at 5 pounds (baby A—Dakota) and 5 pounds 4 ounces (baby B—Montana). "Ironic" because the doctor had wanted to induce me on Friday morning, at thirty-six weeks exactly, because the (inaccurate) ultrasound had said that baby A was more than a pound less than baby B, and he wanted to be sure that baby A was getting enough food. In reality, they were only four ounces apart.

All was well in my world. I smiled to myself as I noted that what I'd asked for repeatedly during my pregnancy—the best labor ever with Dakota and Montana weighing in at at least five pounds each and born four minutes apart—had happened. It had happened! Rock on Deliberate Creation.

Word on the street is that it is a long and arduous recovery from a C-section. Didn't care. Had a spinal and morphine during the surgery? No worries. My sons were healthy, happy, and in my arms, and so it was, in fact, the best labor and delivery ever.

# Chapter 28

# The Deliberately Created C

*"We all possess more power and greater
possibilities than we realize, and visualizing is one
of the greatest of these powers."*
*- Genevieve Behrend*

I privately and secretly wanted a C-Section during my entire pregnancy with my twins, but admitted it to no one. It seems odd to say this now, but it's true. There's a reason why, and it has to do with the Law of Attraction.

Before I was pregnant with the twins Philippe and I were telling our friend Dianne how we really wanted twins and were manifesting them (utilizing the three Practices), and she told us the heartbreaking and tragic story of her friend who had had twins and had an awful thing happen at their birth. She delivered the first twin vaginally and then there were complications so they rushed her—without her husband—into an emergency C-Section. Unbeknownst to her or her husband (she was "under" and her husband wasn't in the OR), her second son lost oxygen during the birth and was stillborn. The birthing team resuscitated the baby but never told his parents. Six weeks later at her son's checkup the doctor said that her son has suffered severe brain damage and would be a vegetable for life. Her other twin son was totally healthy.

There was a long silence after Dianne told us this story. As Philippe and I tried to process the horrendous story she'd just told us, Dianne asked herself silently (she later told me) why on earth she had just told us the story. I then broke the silence, turned to Philippe and said, "If I ever get pregnant with twins, I'm having a C-Section."

When I did get pregnant with Dakota and Montana, none of us breathed a word about the tragic story of Dianne's friend's twins. I didn't speak of the story again or even think about it because I know well the power of the Law of Attraction and Deliberate Creation. I know that what I think and talk about comes about and I that worrying is using my imagination to create something that I don't want. But from the moment I saw my positive pregnancy test with Dakota and Montana, I knew that I wanted and would create a safe, healthy, fun, and successful C-Section.

I never breathed a word to my midwives, doctors, friends, or family. Or even Dianne. Not a word. But all the while, I was manifesting a C, utilizing the three Practices. It's most powerful to manifest when you keep your wish to yourself, so this manifestation gained a lot of momentum for nine months. I could've gone the traditional route of simply scheduling a C-Section, citing my friend's friend's tragic story as my reason, but my heart and intuition guided me to create it as I did, silently utilizing the three Practices.

The afternoon before I went into labor my twin baby boys were both head down and ready to deliver vaginally but I had faith that the Universe would take care of my wish.

Then, as you may recall, when I arrived at the hospital in labor, my midwife told her nurse that Montana, baby B, was in "an interesting position." Indeed, he'd done a 180 in the last twelve hours since my last ultrasound. A C-Section was therefore mandated, performed safely and successfully, and this Super-mom got her wish, down to the weight of her baby boys and the number of minutes between their births. Thank you Universe! Utilizing the three Practices works. Sometimes (oftentimes) it all comes together in the last few moments (or hours), so have faith. And let go.

# Chapter 29

# Why I'm Not Homeschooling Anymore

*"The mediocre teacher tells. The good teacher explains. The superior teacher demonstrates. The great teacher inspires."*
*- William Arthur Ward*

We homeschooled our kids for two years. As you may recall from Chapter 26, on September 4, 2009 I did a pregnancy test and was overjoyed to find out that I was pregnant with twins. On the very same day we opened our restaurant and began homeschooling. All in one day.

My Spirit tends to work that way. It queues things up and then when the energy is lined up everything happens–at once, as often is the case when you're utilizing the three Practices.

So in similar fashion, on that fateful day in July 2011 when we chose joyfully to not be a label anymore, we also chose to send our children to public school and to sell our restaurant (more on why we sold our restaurant in Chapter 30).

I was ambivalent about homeschooling from day one. At times I was thrilled about it and other times it didn't feel right. Usually if something doesn't feel right I jump off the train, and fast. My intuition is strong and I always listen to it. Why not with the homeschooling? My husband was gung ho. This was an odd experience because we usually agree on everything. With my first husband it wasn't like that at all. We agreed on very little (but loved each other very much). So to have this one thing that we weren't on the same page on lead me to say to myself, "I can be right, or I can be happy." So I let it go, again and again. Oh I brought it up to my husband many times—that I was ambivalent. Sister speaks her mind. But in the end I'd sigh and say, "Well, OK. If you really feel that way."

So why, on that fateful and amazing day in July 2011, when we joyfully decided to stop being a label and sell our restaurant, did I say to Philippe," There's one more thing," to which he responded, "Not the homeschooling?" "Yes, the homeschooling." I said with love. "But why?" he asked, knowing it was done—he'd seen that look on my face before.

I can't be 20 eight year-old kids for Sagey (now age eight). I can't be 20 five-year-old kids for Phoenix (now age five). No matter how much I love them and how hard I try, this I can't do. Are the academics superior when we homeschool? Absolutely. On any given homeschool day Sagey and Phoenix would be done with their academics by 9 am and have the whole day to play and explore. And they quickly moved a grade ahead. Did I care about this at that point? No.

Here's why. I did get my M.Ed. at Teachers College at Columbia in 1994, but it was in Psychology, not in early childhood education, because I never intended on teaching preschool, kindergarten, or 1st grade. I love to teach, but not in that way. That's not my dharma. I wished for my kids that they could show up to a classroom every morning to a teacher who was doing her dharma–who had lesson plans and a colorful happy classroom and years of teaching experience. But most of all, a room full of kids my child's age.

So in my experience of two years homeschooling, you just can't replicate the classroom as a homeschooler. Oh I tried. I did some serious damage at AC Moore and Michaels and The Learning Center getting the best classroom supplies ever. I wrote our day out on a big dry erase board every night. But it just ain't the same. The kids, the energy, the playground, the bell, the lockers, the classroom, the homeroom teacher, and the "lunch lady" were missing.

My family needed to live the homeschool experience for two years for my husband and I to really get it. To really see. To know deep in our hearts what's the best ever for our plus five. And to truly appreciate, to truly have gratitude for our children's amazing preschool and elementary school teachers. For all they do and continue to do day in and day out to show up for their students in the sparkly way they do. On the second day of Sagey's first term back to school, as I dropped her off to second grade, her teacher said to me, "Yesterday was pure bliss." And Sister meant it.

So it ain't about better or worse. It's about what's best for our family of seven. It's about what my Spirit was gently guiding me toward. It was great that we homeschooled for two years to have the awareness and gratitude for our amazing public school system, but also so Sagey and Phoenix could spend all day every day of that time with their new twin baby brothers and with each other. They bonded amazingly during those two years at home, a bond for a lifetime. Our now fourteen year-old chose to continue to go to public middle school while we homeschooled and was mostly happy she did, but at times felt left out because the other plus four were together 24/7.

The Universe made it abundantly clear that our decision was the right one on that first day back to school. Sagey and I walked to her elementary school joyfully hand in hand and were greeted by so many kind, shiny, welcoming faces—students, parents, teachers, and more. "Welcome to school!" and "Where did you move from?" Or "I love your yoga studios!" or "How did you like homeschooling?" or "I love your blogs!" etc. The love and magic was palpable. My heart grew two sizes bigger.

Then as I was leaving, a sweet young woman, probably a teachers aide I guessed, smiled at me and said, "I love your class! I come every Sunday. I love Prana. I've tried other studios and none compare. It's the energy."

I smiled, thanked her, and then noticed a big poster next to her on the wall with her picture on it. I squinted my eyes to read it (my LASIK wore off) and it said, "Welcome to Underwood," and under those words were the principle's name. This sweet woman who was talking about yoga, energy, and Prana Power Yoga was the principal, not a teacher's aide. Thank you, Universe!

Ommmmmm.

Chapter 30

Chapter 30

# Why We Sold
# Our Restaurant

"Everything that has a beginning has an ending.
Make your peace with that and all will be well."
- Buddha

PHOTO: MEGAN GEORGE

Sometimes our path turns out differently than we had planned. Often times our path turns out differently than we had planned. The yoga (Practice one) is to notice when the Universe is asking us to let go and move on, and having the grace and integrity to do so for the highest good of all.

I teach and write all day every day about Deliberate Creation (Practice two) and I utilize it all the time. I believe in it and I have many blessings in my abundant life to reflect how the Law of

Attraction works. However, for the two years that we owned our restaurant, I wasn't seeing what I was looking at. I couldn't see what was right in front of me. One thing after another pointed to the fact that Philippe and I were paddling upstream big-time with the restaurant; however, we couldn't see the signs and not-so-subtle clues from the Universe. I won't go through every event and situation because there were so many, but suffice it to say, it felt like pushing a boulder. And this is not how my life usually flows. I know better and consistently utilize the three Practices of creating the best life ever. But I so believed in educating the community about the benefits of eating high vibration raw vegan foods and creating and offering a place to eat healthy delicious food that I ignored my higher self and intuition.

Philippe and I put our hearts, souls, energy, and a ton of money into building out our Prana Restaurant from scratch. The build out alone ended up costing double what we thought it would cost, and it didn't end there. Checks were constantly needed to pay for the food, the labor, more dehydrators, more tables, more juicers, more blenders, etc. Whatever profit came into Prana Power Yoga was immediately poured into our restaurant. Yet no profits were seen. My kids had wanted to buy a swing set for two years but we paid the vendors and the restaurant staff instead. We had intended on starting the build-out of our Prana Brooklyn studio for months, as we had already begun paying rent in Brooklyn and our manager's salary, but the restaurant trumped it every week.

"The restaurant business is tough," we'd been warned. Many people had told us we were crazy to open a restaurant. "No one understands how rough the restaurant business is 'till they experience it first-hand," said one of our Prana students who owns two restaurants. "You're nuts to do this Taylor. Don't do it!" I smiled and we stuck to our plan and dream of bringing healthy delicious food to Newton Corner, Massachusetts, and finally having a local raw vegan place to eat at after seven years of being raw vegan.

Our first chef Stuart, bless his heart, told us that we'd lose money year one. "All restaurants do!" he warned us. "Oh no, not us," I thought. "We'll be different."

We weren't.

So the money wasn't flowing well, or at all, but the kicker was that no matter how much time, money, love, and energy we put into our restaurant, it seemed that everyone was mad at us. A strange thing to say (so not Deliberate Creation), but that was the energy. And I know energy. This was palpable! An energy that I was not used to and that was not the best ever. The customers were mad because it was "too expensive." Meanwhile, I knew that we weren't even making a profit because the food and labor costs were so high. Our Prana Restaurant staff never seemed to be happy. There was tension. An edge. We loved them so much and wanted everyone to be joyful and abundant but it just wasn't flowing that way.

We had never ever intended on living at the restaurant, on being there all the time. With five kids (including our twins who were infants at the time), four yoga studios, building another yoga studio—or intending to—and my writing and consulting, we knew that it wasn't our dharma to be there all the time, so our intention was to hire the best people ever to run it successfully, bring the best food ever to the community, and enjoy it ourselves. But this wasn't happening. Why was it so hard? I kept meditating on it being easy and stayed positive (Practice two) no matter how it was wearing Philippe, our family, and me down day in and day out.

Then in early July 2011 as we settled in with our five kids on Nantucket to unwind and enjoy each other's company away from the stresses of a restaurant that was exhausting us mentally, emotionally, and financially, I heard Philippe swear out loud as he looked at the computer. This was the first time I'd ever heard him say this word in all the years we've been together. "What is it?" I asked. "We have to wire seven thousand dollars to the restaurant," he explained.

That was the moment. It was then that we both knew it was time to let go. In that moment, we let go of the oars and began paddling downstream (Deliberate Creation).

We believed so passionately in the healing properties of raw vegan food that we had been ignoring all of the Universal signals to move on, but in that moment, it all became clear. The Universe had showed us the door on several occasions but we had stayed in our minds and ignored it, an example of what not to do when utilizing Practice two. When you Deliberately Create, it's essential to listen to your intuition, to the Universe, and to see the clues laid out before you. There will always be clues. There will always be synchronicities, divininely sent. You must be awake and aware to see them. Practicing yoga helps you to cultivate this awareness and stay on the path.

So finally, after two years, our Spirits spoke, we surrendered, and enormous relief and joy followed. As will happen every time you make a decision that keeps you on the path toward creating the best life ever.

We have absolutely no regrets, don't believe in mistakes, and are grateful that we were able to plant the seeds of the raw vegan community in Newton Corner for two years. We were excited to pass the baton to the new owners, divinely sent to us within a week of our decision to sell, and continuing to offer healthy, delicious food to the community. We magnetized owners who are giving the restaurant and the community all the love and energy they deserve.

Although pouring a lot of money into the restaurant and seeing no profit was a real issue and a bummer, we sold the restaurant because of the exhausting energetics of it all. All the paddling upstream. All the projections. All the drama. We didn't want to be the "mean bosses" and the "mean parents" anymore. We loved our Prana Restaurant family and knew they were doing their best, as were we, but it seemed that no matter what we did or said, that palpable tension was there. No matter how positive and loving we were. No matter how much money we continued to pour into the restaurant. Where was the gratitude and love and transformational energy that envelops our yoga studios? Where was that beautiful, easy, and joyful energy? All of these dynamics were sure-bet clues that we were not doing our dharma—that we were not on our path of the best life ever, that we were not in the flow of the Universe, as you are when you Deliberately Create, when you consistently utilize all three Practices concurrently. This is a great example of how we all live, learn, try, and try again. It's not about being perfect and not falling down. It's about utilizing the three Practices in a disciplined and fun way to create your best life ever and when you don't, stopping, noticing, shifting, dusting yourself off, and beginning again. As I talk about in Chapter 11, it's never too late to begin again.

The lessons? There are always lessons. Be mindful to stop and take them in on your journey. This is an important part of Deliberate Creation. By living some contrast, we learn what we don't want, so we know more clearly what we do want. It's as simple as that. You don't need to live a lot of contrast, but you will live some. Always. To know what it is that you do want. I suggest you keep your contrast to a minimum. And you can. Remember, you're creating your life, every moment. You have this power. You've always had this power.

The lessons we learned were many. We learned that there is a difficult and stressful energy in the restaurant business and therefore, a lot of drama and turnover—two things that are so not Philippe and me. And "this" is why restaurants are so tough. Our Spirits are now choosing to learn and grow through joy and love, and paddle downstream.

We learned that to own a restaurant, you really need to live there 24/7, which again, was never our intention. Our kids come first and we have five yoga studios and I am a writer and teacher at heart. But it just don't work if you ain't there. This is why chef owned restaurants (usually) do well.

After we sold our restaurant we felt immense relief and excitement since we were able to once again turn all of our creative energy toward our five children, five yoga studios, and my writing.

So remember, the Universe is never subtle and always lets us know when we are on the path. Even when you've been ignoring its signals for a long time. It's never too late to hear the call, and begin again.

# Chapter 31

# My Top 7 Tips For Getting Stuff Done

PHOTO: MEGAN GEORGE

"All power is from within and therefore under our control."
- Robert Collier

People often ask how I do everything that I do. The answer is simple. Most things are. I utilize the three Practices every day. And you will too, after reading this book and practicing doing so. It's gonna be easy. I'm excited and happy for you.

I'm still gonna give you my list of top 7 tips to get stuff done, but before I do, let me tell you that the alternate title of this chapter is not, "I'm great and here's why." My message with this chapter and this book is that you too can do this! Anyone can.

"A mind at peace, a mind centered and not focused on harming others, is stronger than any physical force in the Universe."
- Wayne Dyer

Tip #1: Center yourself before you do anything.

This includes having a conversation. This includes writing an email. This includes eating a meal. This includes taking a shower. I mean anything. Your method of centering is personal to you. Everything is. For me, it's yoga and any type of movement. That's how I'm wired. If you're wired to feel centered by a seated meditation, rock on. If you feel grounded after cleaning, get out the broom and swiffer. If reading centers you, crack open that book or newspaper. You get the idea. "Just do it," to borrow a brilliant phrase from an athletic company, and just as brilliant, "This is how I do it." By being centered before you do or say anything, you will be incredibly efficient. People will stare and ask, "how DO you do all that you do and stay happy most of the time to boot?"

"Just Play. Have Fun. Enjoy the Game."
- Michael Jordan

Tip #2:

Get happy. In any way you can. Follow your bliss.

"But wait," you ask, "I want to know how to get stuff done, Taylor. Fun is for the weekends." Not so. Fun is for now. And as you create joy in your life, your efficiency will skyrocket. Skyrocket! "How and why?" You ask.

Because of the Law of Attraction. Whatever you put out comes right back—immediately. Right now. The time is NOW. So put out joy, feel it, be it, and the Universe will synchronize events so everything flows beautifully and easily (read: efficiently). One who is connected to the stream is more powerful and efficient than millions who are not.

"It's all about the power of the focus of your mind."
- Abraham-Hicks

Tip #3: Ignore some stuff.

Become a master at discipline. Discipline is remembering what you want. It's not possible for you to do every single thing that comes onto your path. So ask yourself, "What's my intention?" Keep asking yourself this question and if the task at hand is lined up with that intention.

When I say, "Ignore some stuff," I'm referring to the tasks that aren't in line with your intention—and also thoughts about anything that you don't want or like. This is called distraction. Your mind will do whatever it can to distract you and resist. Ignore it and focus on what you do want. Your job is to allow (in line with Deliberate Creation). You will become so good at this—a master! Just practice, practice, practice.

"I've discovered that numerous peak performers use the skill of mental rehearsal or visualization. They mentally run through important events before they happen."
- Charles A. Garfield

Tip #4: Visualize.

See what you want before you begin any action. Whatever you see materialized on the earth plane was first a thought and a visualization. You don't create with your action but with your thoughts and visualizations. So see it! If you can't see it, how can the Universe?

"Act as if what you intend to manifest in life is already a reality. Feel the essence of it. Eliminate thoughts of conditions, limitations, or the possibility of it not manifesting. If left undisturbed in your mind and in the mind of intention simultaneously, it will germinate in the physical world."
- Wayne Dyer

Tip #5: Feel the essence of it.

Feel the essence of whatever it is that you want. Feel what it will feel like to be efficient with ease. For everything to line up beautifully and easily. To get a lot of stuff done quickly and joyfully. Feel it. Then watch it materialize.

"Enthusiasm is excitement with inspiration, motivation, and a pinch of creativity."
- Bo Bennett

Tip #6: Only act from inspiration. Then multitask with joy. It will be easy when you are inspired.

"I never did a day's work in my life. It was all fun."
- Thomas A. Edison

Tip #7: Only do what you love.

Perhaps you're saying, "I don't love my job but I have to pay the bills Sister."

I hear ya.

So here's what you do to create your perfect job. In each moment, find something on which to focus that you do love. It's there. Find it. Now focus on it.

The Law of Attraction will then bring more like it into your experience. It is law.

Then synchronicities will line up to create a job you love. Pretty darn fast if you aren't resistant. And when you're doing what you love, you get stuff done quickly and easily.

# Chapter 32

# Jealousy

The Law of Attraction is responding to you.

Have you ever been jealous? Envious? From the definitions I've read of the two words, it appears that envy is slightly less harmful than jealousy, but I'm gonna explain why neither is behooving you.

When you're jealous, you're lowering your energy and vibration demonstrably. And your energy, mood, thoughts, and words are what magnetize people, events, and circumstances to you in each moment.

You figure out something that you want, you focus on it, and then it shows up in your life, being driven by someone else. The Universe is toying with you. It's showing you—yes, you can have this thing, but how badly do you want it? Do you really believe you can have it or are you pretending to believe but not really feeling the essence of what you desire?

If you can smile and feel exhilaration for that person living your dream, you will jump immediately into their Vortex of creation where anything is possible. Imagine that! You are riding that wave of Prana ("life force" in Sanskrit)!

But if you move into jealousy, you won't. In fact, you'll move down the emotional scale so low as to guarantee that that thang won't be showing up anytime soon. So how do you do it? How do you stop those green feelings from appearing?

Practice, practice, practice. Truly take in and live the fact that the reality of this Universe is abundance, not scarcity. Scarcity is not real. It's a fear-based mentality that has been perpetuated for centuries on this planet. All those who've been incredible creators didn't buy into the (erroneous) scarcity mentality. They knew that abundance was and is everyone's birthright. They knew that there is more than enough for everyone, and that them winning didn't mean that anyone else lost.

To be jealous means you think that someone over there is doing well to the detriment of you. It means you think there isn't enough to go around. But the reality is that there is more than enough (abundance!) for all, and that when you see someone doing well, it's proof that the Law of Attraction and Deliberate Creation are at work. Be happy for her! Be inspired by him! Be observant—watch how she moves through the world. Watch his thoughts, his words, his actions. Feel her energy. Ask him how he does it. He'll happily tell you because he knows that you creating what you want is the best thing ever. Abundance means that everyone wins!

So go ahead, give it a try. The next time you feel that awful feeling (jealousy always feels bad), let it go and reassure yourself that you can be, do, and have anything that you want. And so can she. And so can he. More power to all to create the best life and the best planet together—one thought, one dream, one visualization at a time.

# Chapter 33

# The Rebel

*"Anything that is your object of attention when you're happy benefits from the infusion of your well-being."*
*-.Abraham-Hicks*

I have thought and done things differently for as long as I can remember. This trait, with which I walked onto this Earth, coupled with a desire to please others, which I learned on this Earth very early on during a rough childhood, resulted in tension, and therefore, suffering.

It's been my experience that many people can relate to this. You see and do things differently than the mainstream, but want to please others, and so tension and suffering result.

Oftentimes we aren't even aware of the tension—the suffering. We walk our path in a tremendous amount of pain but hide it from others, especially ourselves. And it works—for a while. Until it doesn't anymore, and we get sick, tired, depressed, angry, bored, confused, and lost. Our Spirit cannot stay quiet for long and so the symptoms begin. The symptoms that beg—please listen, please see, please be aware, please be mindful, and then, please make a shift. A shift towards joy and following your heart. A shift towards your path.

I used to be in a relationship where many things I did, said, and thought were questioned, laughed off or at, or, in the worst case, pathologized. Sometimes it was "only" energetic or a roll of the eyes. But I felt it and oh, so did my Spirit. And like little pieces of confetti, it built up over time.

In time, I knew in my heart that although I loved my partner very much and he loved me, this was no way to live. After many years, it became unbearable and I felt as though I couldn't breathe. I felt as though I was living in a prison. But I had created this prison and so only I had the key out.

Yoga helped me to see the prison I had created and to take responsibility for it, as well as for my choices and decisions. Yoga lifted the veil of illusion under which I had been living for years.

Yoga did not cause my first marriage to end, as my ex-husband sometimes surmised at the beginning of the end of our union. Yoga helped me to remember who I am. Yoga helped me to end the suffering I was enduring and therefore causing others to endure, unnecessarily. When we suffer, we cause others to suffer. When we are in joy, we help others to feel joy. It's all energetic. It's all about vibration.

There's no right or wrong energy or vibration, just different ones. As Abraham-Hicks says, "You cannot be a leader to those who are not vibrating at your level," nor can you abide easily and lovingly beside those who are on a completely different energetic level.

But how do you know? What does vibration mean? How does it feel to spend the majority of your time around those who are not vibrating where you are? Exhausting. Frustrating. Annoying. Suffocating. Like a prison. Anything but joy.

This is not about judgment. This is not about placing blame. This is about energy. And the flow of the Universe. If something isn't flowing, it's not on your path, so let it go. Move on and bless and send light to those people, places, and things that you "leave behind."

You actually never really "leave anyone or anything behind." Everyone with whom you've ever had a relationship will always be a part of you. No relationship ever ends. Ever. Not through death or divorce or simply losing touch.

So celebrate the "different" or "rebellious" way about you and be proud of who you are and the path you walk. Walk it with integrity, grace, and courage, speaking your truth with love and compassion. And when things shift in your life (as they will because change and growth are inevitable), when there isn't an energetic fit anymore, send light and love and move on. So that all beings on this planet can walk their paths with the passion and joy that we were all born with.

# Chapter 34

# The "Tween"

Your thought determines how
people in your life behave.

A few years ago we went through a year when our now fourteen-year-old was a "tween." All of my Super-mom friends who had gone through the "tween stage" warned me in no uncertain terms, "Oh, just wait. Just wait till she's twelve. What a nightmare. You know how tweens are. You remember what you were like when you were twelve."

I didn't, and I don't. I wasn't your "typical" tween. In fact, back in the day, tween wasn't even a term yet. But even if it had been, I wasn't pushing the boundaries with my parents. I knew better. I was surviving in my home, one moment at a time.

My parents used to say (in their moments of non-craziness, which could come at any time, or not), "We don't feel right making boundaries with you because you're so hard on yourself. You don't need any rules."

Of course I didn't need rules. They were set in stone in my unconscious at a very young age: "Do this. Look like that. Achieve this. Be perfect, or else. And don't tell (about what really happens in our home...or else)." Yes, indeed, "rules" were unnecessary at this point.

So achieve I did. Attempt perfection I did. Tell I didn't. I simply channeled all the pain and fear into "acceptable" and "honorable" things like studying and achieving and being the best athlete I could be. At age twelve I was living with Nick Bollettieri in Florida to train to be a tennis pro, a year before The Nick Bolletieri Tennis Academy was born. I was happy to do so because I felt safe there and unsafe at home. I wasn't whining that I wanted to go to the mall. I wasn't texting my parents from the mall saying I wanted to stay an extra two hours and then could they pick up my friends and me at 9 pm and take us out to dinner?

You didn't push boundaries at Nick's. Once I did, and oh, I remember it vividly. It's unusual for me to remember anything from my childhood well if at all since most of it is blocked out thanks to repression. Repression allows abused children to survive and function day-to-day.

At Nick's we weren't allowed to listen to the radio or watch TV; however, there was a TV in my roommates' and my room. Somehow I'd gotten wind of the fact that "Rocky," my all time favorite film, was on TV that night, and I wasn't gonna miss it. I finished all of my chores (including cleaning Nick's shower with a toothbrush and doing his laundry) and my homework and we turned off our lights to ostensibly go to sleep. A few minutes later, I stole out of our bunk bed, turned on the TV, and watched a few minutes of Rocky, with the volume down so low that I was lip-reading.

SLAM! Our bedroom door flew open and there was Nick. I was terrified and shaking. Nick was not happy. I was punished for weeks, doing extra chores, extra calisthenics, running extra miles, but none of that mattered to me as much as the look in Nick's eyes when he opened that door. His disappointment and anger were palpable and shook me to my core.

Fast-forward to 2010. Madison Leigh, age twelve at the time, was doing her thing, growing up and learning about the Universe through the eyes and experiences of many—her family, her friends, her teachers, and people with whom she comes into contact day to day.

I wasn't looking for or expecting any "typical" tween behavior because I honestly didn't know what that was (both from my own twelve-year-old experience and from reading about what "typical" tweens "are like" because I purposefully didn't read that stuff since it had nothing to do with my daughter and my reality). So I didn't see it. What I did experience was a graceful, loving, sweet, smart, kind, maternal girl who I'm honored to have as my daughter.

A girl who does her homework on her own and gets it in on time unbeknownst to me, because she wants to, not because she is scared not to (as I was).

A girl who helped her little brother feel included when his (then) five-year-old sister and her friend went squealing up the stairs to play "Princess" in her room.

A girl who forgot to practice the piano and told me so honestly, asking if I thought we should skip her lesson that week.

A girl who forgot to hang her coat up and put her boots in the boot drawer just about every time she came into the house, as I secretly smiled through my annoyance, because I knew that she didn't feel the need to be perfect.

A girl who always "spaced" taking off her shoes when she needed to run up to her room to get something she'd forgotten, not abiding by the "no shoes in the house" rule, annoying both Philippe and me but, again, giving me a sense of relief since I knew she wasn't afraid of us. I believe that no child should fear his or her parent. They should respect and honor him and her, but without fear.

There are always two things to feel in any moment—love or fear. What are you and your tween feeling now, in this moment? During this "power struggle?" What's really going on? Have you chosen love or fear? Does it have to do with them, you, or something that you read "is going to happen?"

The more you practice yoga, the more you will choose love—again and again (Deliberate Creation)—and not listen to "the authorities." YOU are the authority. This is your life and your creation. Your Deliberate Creation.

The more you practice yoga, the more you will be cognizant of your reactions, or, more accurately, your responses. When you react you are "re-acting"—acting again from a previous experience. You are not in the present. When you respond, you are in the NOW. Where all of your power is.

So tune into your power and enjoy your child—whatever his or her age—for whoever he or she is, letting go of the stereotypes of what "that age" is like. This is your life. This is your reality. Create it as you wish, utilizing the three Practices to create the best life ever.

# Chapter 35

# The Eating Disorder

*"I love and approve of myself."*
*- Louise Hay*

When I was in college I had an eating disorder. I remember the day it started. I'd quit the Brown tennis team and was feeling lost. My whole life I'd been "an athlete." I'd seen myself and been seen by others in this way. And good thing, too, because I'd channeled all the pain and fear I'd had as a child into sports, and it worked well for me. At age five I was a figure skater. Years later, when the skating rink in Lake Bluff, Illinois burned down (or so my parents told me), I became a competitive tennis player. I trained hard and went to live with Nick Bollettieri at age twelve, hoping to turn pro. I lived at Nick's for a year and then returned to our new home in Calabasas, California to attend high school (we'd since moved from the Midwest), with the intention of achieving more balance in my life.

I played number one on my high school tennis team, won States every year, played tournaments on the weekends, and lived mostly like a "normal" teenager. I was social, had fun, went to parties, and was named Homecoming Queen in my senior year.

Fast forward to the day I quit the team at Brown. I was talking to one of my best friends and said to her, "I don't know who I am. I've always been an athlete. Now who am I?" She had a great one-liner response that made me both laugh and reflect (I wish I remembered it because it was good). And the "rest of my life" began.

I actually loved not playing tennis anymore. I loved the freedom and the extra time I had with my friends and to do other things and activities I'd never had time for. Life was good.

Until the fateful day when my eating disorder was born. That day when I got on the scale at the athletic center. I noted my weight, and the next time I was about to eat a chocolate chip muffin as a snack, I thought twice. "If I don't eat this, maybe I'll lose weight. Maybe I'll be skinnier," I mused.

The pain and grief from the abuse during my childhood was stirring. It had nowhere to go now—nowhere to be channeled—since I was no longer whacking a tennis ball two to five hours a day and grunting loudly every single time I hit it. That energy had to go somewhere. And so my mind, brilliant as all of our minds are, found a place for it to go. My mind felt it wouldn't behoove me to have and own the painful memories kept at bay by years of sports and achievement and constantly pushing myself. Not just yet. Now was a time for fun—for making friends for a lifetime and wonderful memories I'd always cherish.

So my mind hooked onto the next best thing—distracting itself from the past by thinking and obsessing about my body and my weight. There's certainly a lot of support and encouragement out there to help an eating and body image disorder along and keep it goin'. It's an epidemic.

I didn't eat that chocolate chip muffin. And I began to be aware of and restrict other treats as well. The next time I was at the athletic center, my weight on the scale made me smile, and an addict was born. I was addicted to the control, the results, the responses of others. "Wow! You've lost weight! You look great!" Or, "Are you OK? You're losing a lot of weight." It didn't matter what they said—as long as they noticed. My clothes didn't fit anymore. I was elated. I felt powerful—the exact opposite of the powerlessness I'd felt as a child.

I'd always been a "big eater," always had a good appetite. I'd never been picky, always eating whatever was on my plate. So "not eating" wasn't an option for me. My metabolism wouldn't allow it. What I did instead was become obsessed with what I ate, choosing those things that I could eat abundantly and still lose weight. Huge salads containing only veggies and watered down diet dressing, plain bagels, plain pancakes, and low-fat frozen yogurt. Back in the day, the whole "carb" thing wasn't in yet—it was all about "low cal" and "low fat."

Instead of being afraid of what I was really afraid of—the memories that haunted the very depths of my mind—I became afraid of foods that were high in calories or fat. I began to alter my activities to avoid those foods and people who'd try to "force" me to eat them. I lost all connection to my body. It was all about how my jeans fit and what the scale said—which I stepped onto with bated breath every single morning (by now I'd bought my own for privacy and convenience). My friends and boyfriend grew concerned. "They're jealous," my demented mind rationalized.

I'd lost touch with reality. My grades didn't suffer. My social life didn't suffer. But my Spirit did. I had no freedom. I was living in a prison, which I'd created.

There were so many other women engaging in the same behavior that it was almost commonplace at Brown at that time. We all had our different idiosyncrasies but overall, we were all doing the same thing. The difference was I had a fierce discipline (learned from my abusive childhood and my year at Nick Bollettieri's) that meant I never fell "off the weight loss wagon." I never "cheated." Never.

Years later, when my ex-husband's sister—also my best friend at the time—was talking to me about how hard it was for me to "let go" and "just enjoy a cookie," I explained it to her like this, "Imagine that you eat a cookie, and then someone beats the **** out of you for twelve hours after your last bite. You probably wouldn't eat that cookie ever again, right?" I was the person beating the **** out of myself for the twelve hours after eating the cookie. I was the one creating my prison, as we all do. We all create our own pain and our own prisons. Once you can accept this, you will understand the amazing power you have. Right now! To create whatever you want. The way outta that prison is only a thought away, utilizing Deliberate Creation.

I did find the way out. I did find the thought that lead me to my path to freedom. I did heal from my eating disorder. Then, at a point in my life when my mind knew I could take the time and energy to face my past and heal from it, I had, faced, and dealt with my childhood memories.

For a time, as I struggled with the inevitable pain and grief that surfaced with the memories, my eating disorder resurfaced. But as I walked the path of healing and my Spirit felt freed by speaking the truth of my childhood and wonderful people around me heard my truth and believed and supported me, I reclaimed my self and my life. And my eating normalized for good. It's never about the food. Never.

Once healed, I realized that before I had messed up my eating to run from my painful past, I had been proud of my big appetite—both for food and for the many amazing adventures of life. It felt good to feel proud of that again instead of feeling pain or guilt if I ate something that was previously "forbidden." I felt a sense of relief, pride, joy, and power, similar to what you will feel when you utilize the third Practice of creating the best life ever. The power I felt wasn't about the food, of course. It was about reclaiming my life force—my Prana—that had been dormant for those years of food deprivation. It was about the freedom so essential to creating the best life ever.

I'm sharing my eating disorder history so that you know that it's possible to heal wholly and completely from an eating disorder, no matter how deeply rooted it is in the past and no matter how much it's serving you in this moment. Mine did serve me in certain ways at the time, and once I was able to heal what it was holding back, it was no longer necessary.

So don't listen to the "statistics" and the "authorities" on this subject. If you want to heal from your eating disorder you can and you will. When you're ready. Utilizing yoga and Deliberate Creation will help a lot. And once it's healed, you can experience the exhilarating freedom of utilizing the third Practice of creating the best life ever.

Only you can choose to heal yourself. Make the choice, and claim the freedom, joy, and power that is your birthright.

Chapter 36

# The Eleventh Hour: Can You Stay Calm In A Difficult Moment?

Everything is lined up perfectly.

PHOTO: KELLY LORENZ

We had just finished teaching the first weekend of our six-weekend Prana Power Yoga 2007 Teacher Training. It was magical. It was wonderful. It was beyond what I visualized in my mind's eye. The Universe delivered.

The group was spectacular, the Prana was flowing, years of fear and pain were being released, and teachers were being born.

Training was to begin at 8 am on Friday morning and we had lined everything up perfectly. Our three children would spend the twelve-hour training days with my sister, who was flying in from New Mexico. She was helping us out because our (then) six-month-old baby boy Phoenix had never been without me for more than a few hours, while I was teaching or taking a class at Prana.

Our brand-new studio in Cambridge's Central Square would be finished—the tile, wood floors, and heating system in, the walls painted.

Then, in the 11th hour, things began to unravel, or not go according to "plan." My sister wasn't coming. The special order tiles and hardwood floors weren't in. The space wasn't finished. Things were not flowing well, or at all. So on the day before Teacher Training began, I really lived my yoga. How would I respond to this difficult moment?

As my children watched me on the phone with our contractor, I spoke clearly, concisely, and calmly, describing "plan B." They learned a lot in that moment. Would anger help the situation? Fear? What was I teaching my children?

Once "plan B" for the studio space was clarified, we moved on to the issue of child-care, and decided that our Cambridge studio manager and her nine-month-old son would spend the day playing with our children. Whew! Everything was all set, so the kids and I headed to our (then) ten-year-old's camp dance, while my husband was attending a community meeting.

En route to the dance my cell phone rang. It was our Cambridge studio manager telling me that her nine-month-old son was vomiting everywhere. I felt such compassion for my friend and her son, knowing what it's like when a baby is sick. The whole world stops. Then I asked The Universe, "What next?" My higher self simply said, "Let go." My mind argued, but my Spirit took over. I completely surrendered, went to the camp dance, and danced with my three children to 80's tunes—my six-month-old son on my hip, squealing with delight.

After "My Sharona" ended, it came to me—"Victoria!" My good friend who lives in Cambridge near our new studio could hang out with our kids while we taught. I picked up my cell phone, and her number was already up on the screen. Coincidence? I don't believe in 'em.

Victoria came through, agreeing without hesitation to help us out while we taught. The brand new studio space ended up being just fine—shining in its own "raw" way, sans floors, bathroom tiles, and running water. The contractors did just enough to make it all work. We never know what we'll get when we walk in to teach, and it was the perfect physical manifestation of this. A good lesson for our teacher training students.

When I was very young, my tennis coach took me to tennis courts in the "worst" neighborhoods in downtown Chicago. The nets were metal, the pavement cracked, the players angry and sad. I picked up games with these adults—a little girl with blonde ponytails and a racket as big as I was. They'd laugh when I asked them to play, we'd play, I'd win, and they'd get angry. That prepared me for pretty much any tournament situation imaginable. Your mat prepares you for pretty much any life situation imaginable. Have you practiced today?

Chapter 37

# The Car Seat

"A mind is like a parachute.
It doesn't work if it is not open."
- Frank Zappa

When our son Phoenix was five weeks old and sleeping in bed with us, he began to have some symptoms of gas. He'd start making "Eh eh eh" sounds in his sleep and bunch up his legs like he was in pain.

We'd always loved to have our newborns sleep in our bed with us until they could roll over (at about four months) because it was such a precious experience for everyone and was also so much easier for this Super-mom to nurse in the middle of the night. Sometimes I didn't even have to wake up fully to nurse, and there was no getting out of bed, walking to the crib, etc.

That night as baby Phoenix was squirming and "Eh eh eh'ing," Philippe said, "Let's try this," as he put our five-week-old in his car seat next to our bed. He strapped him into his seat and within five seconds the "Eh eh eh" sounds stopped, and Phoenix was fast asleep.

I was dubious, at best. "We always sleep with our babies," I said to my husband. "Is this OK? To have him in there all night?" I continued. "He's fine," soothed Philippe. "Look at him!"

He did seem supremely happy and comfortable, and so I lay down and closed my eyes.

Ten hours (!) later I opened my eyes with a start and jumped out of bed. Phoenix was just waking up next to our bed (in his car seat), and I was stunned as I looked at the clock. "Ten hours? He slept ten hours straight through the night, at five weeks old?" Delirious with joy and the first good night sleep I'd had in four months (I didn't sleep much during my last trimester), I said to Philippe, "You may be on to something!"

Later that day I was reading some Ayurvedic literature and remembered that Ayurvedic medicine recommends that everyone sleep sitting up. The theory is that after eating any "heavy" meal (breast milk would qualify as heavy), it's difficult to sleep lying down, since when you lie down, your digestive system shuts down. So the food (or milk) in your body ferments as you snooze the night away, causing gas, bloating, and discomfort. "Bingo!" I squealed.

That night, and every night after until he grew out of his car seat, Phoenix slept in his car seat next to our bed—straight through the night—for ten or more hours. I never experienced sleep deprivation with baby Phoenix. It was a miracle!

The lesson? There are two.

First, be open-minded to the solution. This is super important as you create the best life ever. Often the solution is right in front of you—the answer to your wishes—but you are so stuck in your ways that you can't see what's right in front of you. When "the solution" came in the form of Philippe doing something totally unconventional, my first response was resistance ("But we always sleep with our babies in our bed when they're this little!"). I softened as the moments passed, looking at my little guy blissfully asleep, and was then open to the solution, which then gave me (and Phoenix) the priceless gift of a good night's sleep. A really easy and fun way to cultivate open-mindedness is yoga. I'm just sayin'.

Second, if you're a Super-mom or Super-dad with a little baby, try this! Try having your baby sleep next to you (or in his or her room if that floats your boat) in his or her car seat. This is the Ayurvedic way and it works. Also, it makes traveling a snap! No crib needed.

# Chapter 38

# The "Media Fast"

## Only do what your Spirit loves.

PHOTO: TAYLOR WELLS

When I had our daughter, Madison, fourteen years ago, I made a big decision—to go on a "media fast." I'd never "fasted" before, but my Spirit made it abundantly clear that this was a great step toward being the best parent I could be to my new baby daughter.

I used to work in the media. I created a journalism major at Brown and worked at a television station as an intern to prepare for my future. As an intern I ran the teleprompter, ran errands, and wrote some stories. I noticed that the producers didn't care if I was a good writer—if the story wasn't violent or negative in some way, it wouldn't run. This was so counter to my dharma that I continued to write stories about hope and joy, which never ran.

Then one fateful day during my senior year, I took the train to the Big Apple to meet with a producer of the CBS evening news—a Brown alum. He was super nice and met with me for awhile to listen to my hopes and dreams, and then we went into the news room where I met Dan Rather and watched the news broadcast from a sound proof booth. I didn't notice the news being aired so much as the people surrounding me in the booth. Their energy was palpable—stressed out and fearful—as they popped ulcer pills and downed coffee and doughnuts with alarming speed. "This is going to be me," I thought to myself, "If or when I 'make it' in fifteen years. These people are at 'the top,' and they are miserable."

After the broadcast, the Brown alum producer had a heart-to-heart talk with me. He told me to rethink my career choice, explaining that he had no friends and his family had long since given up on him because he had no time for anything but the news. His fiancé had recently dumped him. "There's no balance," he explained honestly. "I have no life."

And this guy had "made it."

I cried on the train ride back to Providence, bemoaning all the time and energy I'd put into creating my major. Students from other Ivy League schools made fun of independent concentrations at Brown because to them it seemed like "a joke" to "make up" a major; but it was actually more challenging to do so because you didn't just sign on to be an econ major or whatever and take the classes included under that major. Instead, you had to prove why your particular classes worked together to create your concentration, and how they would help you to be a journalist. And then write a thesis to prove it.

After the tears came a sense of relief. I knew in my heart that the news was not "the news," it was "the old." That people in "high places" were deciding what you and I and everyone who reads media were going to think and talk about, and it wasn't pretty. Again, there was no balance. It had to be dirty, scandalous, and/or violent or it didn't sell and garner ratings. And that wasn't my truth.

So ten years later, as my belly grew large with a new life inside me, I took the leap to let go of all media. Magazines, newspapers, TV—you name it. I made the decision and the commitment to choose and create my own reality—one that focused on the light instead of negativity and fear.

Now, fourteen years later, I haven't looked back. My life and what I've created is proof that it's done me right. Proof that the Law of Attraction is at work every moment and that Deliberate Creation works.

The ultimate irony is that some twenty-four years after that fateful day at CBS, The Boston Herald asked me to write for them. I now happily spread the light and the Prana every single day on the Herald's website and from time to time in their newspaper. On my terms, writing what I choose to write, and maintaining the balance that was so absent that day in that CBS newsroom. I'm grateful to the Herald for allowing me to do so, love my managing editor, and have learned from writing for the Herald that nothing is black and white—even a newspaper. This is another example of utilizing Deliberate Creation, and how you never know when and how something is going to show up in your life.

# Chapter 39

# The Friend

Every time you feel relief you are releasing resistance.

PHOTO: PHILIPPE WELLS

I have a friend who's "let me down" for years. She's never been "the kind of friend that I am"—the "type of friend that I 'expect' her to be." Then one day it occurred to me that it's my expectations that are bringing me suffering regarding this friend, not her actions or lack thereof. It has nothing to do with her.

For years I wondered how she could not call or offer a hand or even connect when I was in need of love or support at various difficult times in my life.

For years, I wondered how she could do things that I considered betrayals or out of integrity and not blink an eye, let alone attempt to explain her actions to me.

For years, I wondered how she could not make the effort to make a plan to stay connected—to go for a walk or grab a bite or go to a movie—and only contact me when she wanted something (usually having to do with money).

But then it hit me. This has nothing to do with her and has everything to do with me. These are my expectations for a "good friend," and she obviously didn't sign up for them, or for friendship as I define it. She is who she is and me beating the drum of "I can't believe she didn't call or help or stay in integrity or respect me or support me" is my issue, and one that is drawing more darkness—and more people like her—into my aura.

It dawned on me that getting upset about these things or having countless "talks" with her (during which she heard nothing I said) about how I felt this way or that way because of what she did or didn't do, was spinning my wheels and a waste of my time and hers.

And even worse, I was actively magnetizing things I don't want (thoughtlessness, lack of integrity, lack of honor and respect, narcissism, and self-centeredness) into my life.

I can't "make" someone be the friend I want him or her to be. They are who they are and either I accept and love them as they are, or I move on. If I attempt to change them, I suffer. It's my choice.

You'd think I would've learned this after eighteen years of attempting to "change" my ex-husband and him attempting to "change" me. Emphasis on attempting. That's quite a learning curve I know but we were young (seventeen when we met at Brown on the first day of freshman orientation), and had a lot to learn. And a lot of growing up to do—together—before we ultimately parted ways.

I still love him as a friend and always will. But now I love him for who he is. I don't ask him to change or be someone else in order for me to love him. We're not married anymore, and so the "need" to change him is gone. Thank the Universe. He's happier, and so am I. Sometimes divorce is a good thing.

So there it was—a flash of clarity that came, not surprisingly, on my mat—allowing the joy and relief that I'd been wanting regarding this particular situation for quite some time. And it was my choice. My decision. It was in my power all along. You and I have that power. In every situation, in every relationship, in every circumstance in our lives.

Now when I hear my friend's name or see her I smile instead of feeling a drop in my stomach. I've accepted her for who she is and let go of the pain and suffering I caused myself by attempting to make her something that she isn't, and will never be. Instead, I focus on those who do love, support, and nourish me in all the ways that my Spirit desires. This is the practice of Deliberate Creation.

# Chapter 40
# The Swimmer

*Have faith that the 'waters' will warm up to you. They will. Give it a chance, and then let go. In just a few "laps" you won't believe the grace with which you are operating.*

PHOTO: PHILIPPE WELLS

I didn't grow up swimming much, if at all. In fact, I wasn't ever "officially" taught to swim, and that, coupled with the fact that I had a near-death under water experience at a very young age, rendered the water quite unappealing. This was inconvenient at best while growing up and continued to be in my adult years. "Everyone" loves to swim and loves the water, so the trepidation I felt when donning a swimsuit wasn't the norm—or so I believed. I had no idea that not everyone felt comfortable in the water. I did my best with what I was dealt, as I've always done, and made little mention of my fear of water. I'd splash around with the best of 'em in the pool or lake in the summertime in my small Midwestern hometown and just assumed that I'd never be a swimmer. I was happy to get by without anyone noticing that I was pretty much terrified.

Fast-forward to my early twenties. My boyfriend's family had a boat. Boating, fishing, and water-skiing on Cape Cod were family traditions. As I'd done many times before, I gritted my teeth and bore it. I didn't wanna be a drag, so I went out on that boat, weekend after weekend, regardless of the fact that I was terrified most of the time. I even taught myself how to water-ski.

I've always been an athlete and I gave myself a pep talk before getting into that chilly ocean water, telling myself that my life jacket would hold me up and it would all be over soon. I felt proud of my water-skiing—more so than anyone would ever know—for it represented me facing one of my biggest fears.

I made little mention of my fear of water.

Many years later, after my boyfriend and I got married, I stopped going out on the boat. I realized that spending most of my weekend terrified while on the water wasn't kosher, and I didn't deserve to put myself through it anymore. So I just said no.

Another eighteen years later, during the summer of 2009, I chose to "say yes" to swimming, but this time, on my terms. Because I wanted to. We were on Nantucket visiting Philippe's parents, and a friend of mine had joined us for a few days. We were at the beach club for an afternoon of sun and fun, and I was inspired as I watched my friend swim laps in the salt-water pool. She swam so effortlessly and beautifully and seemed to really enjoy what she was doing. What a concept!

I decided in that moment to teach myself how to swim. Not to doggy paddle or even do the breaststroke, but to swim freestyle, something I'd always been afraid of doing. I donned a pair of my (then) eleven-year-old's goggles and hit the water, setting the intention of swimming one hundred laps a day until we went back to Boston in a week.

Four days and four hundred laps later, I could swim freestyle. Not gracefully, not effortlessly, but I could do it.

I continued to swim one hundred laps a day until we left for home, and began to enjoy the routine. I loved the meditative quality of my laps, the breathing, the counting, how my mind became super quiet. I felt refreshed, energized, renewed, and curiously tired after swimming laps. I loved it.

When we arrived home to Newtonville, Massachusetts I wanted to continue my daily swim, but where? It was hot and sunny and we drove over to the municipal pool. I walked in, smelled the intense chlorine, and walked out. "I can't swim there," I proclaimed to Philippe and my kids. "There are too many chemicals in the water and it feels toxic to me. Plus there are eight billion people in the pool and it doesn't feel relaxing. How can I swim laps with all of those people in the pool?"

The quiet salt-water pool on Nantucket had spoiled me and now I was at a loss for where to find this tranquility back in Boston. Next stop: Crystal Lake. We live five minutes from a beautiful lake that we love swimming in, but could I swim "laps" in it? I was willing to give it a try. Philippe and I swam to the other side of the lake and back and fell in love. Now this was swimming. And in nature! We continued our daily swim until the waters grew cold in the chilly autumn months, sometimes swimming at the crack of dawn (one of us at a time) to fit it in before our kiddos woke up, and sometimes bringing all three of our kids (the twins weren't born yet) and taking turns doing our "laps" across the lake and back.

The waters grew cold around the same time that my pregnancy test came back with a joyous positive, and so lying on the couch during my first trimester pregnant with twins replaced swimming a half mile in Crystal Lake.

But as my energy returned in my second trimester I longed again for the tranquility I'd found in the water while swimming my laps, and the weightlessness that the water provides, which I knew would feel great when carrying twins.

# I was willing to give it a try.

I searched for a place to swim daily and found it only a few minutes from our home. Our local YMCA. It had always been there—how could I have never partaken? Two pools and the nicest staff ever! I was in.

My laps became effortless and joyful and maybe even graceful (you'll have to ask the lifeguards and other swimmers about that) and the only hesitation I had was that initial "brrrrrr" feeling when I first got into the water. It's amazing to me how the water could feel so cold initially, and then within two laps, feel as warm as butter on hot bread.

One day as I was swimming lap six or seven, it occurred to me that it's a beautiful metaphor for life. Sometimes you just need to "jump in"—to the water or the project or the relationship or the job—and have faith that the "waters" will warm up to you. Because they will. Give it a chance, and then let go. In just a few "laps" you won't believe the grace with which you are operating, utilizing Deliberate Creation to create the best life ever.

# Chapter 41
# He Said/She Said

"Be impeccable with your word. Speak with integrity. Say only what you mean. Avoid using the word to speak against yourself or to gossip about others. Use the power of your word in the direction of truth and love."
- Don Miguel Ruiz

"He said that you said...." "She said that you said.... "I'm so hurt that you said...."

Ever been in the middle of a he said/she said mishap? If not, kudos to you. If so, lemme give you some advice that will help you to create the best life ever.

Years ago, he said/she said gossip made its way into my aura and life a lot more than it does now.

With all of the people I teach and all of the people I consult with and all of the people I see and interact with on a daily basis in our five yoga studios and our five kids' schools, one might say that "he said/she said" is "inevitable." But I'm here to tell ya, it's not.

You have a choice what and whom you draw into your aura and your experience (this is the essence of Deliberate Creation) and here are a few ways to insure that the "he said/she said" silliness stays out of your orbit:

Speak only the truth.

"Love all. Trust a few. Do wrong to none." (Shakespeare)

You have a choice what and whom you draw into your aura and your experience.

When others attempt to engage you in "he said/she said," don't engage. Ideally, change the subject casually. If that don't work say that you're not interested in the dialogue. If that don't work, walk away.

When others come to you and say, "He said that you said this" or "She said you did that" and it's not true, resist the temptation to "defend" yourself. I put "quotations" around defend because you ain't defending nobody. You're wasting your time and energy. People are gonna believe what they want to believe based upon many things that have nothing to do with you. So save your breath and energy for higher purposes, like spreading the light and being of service to others.

When you learn that others have said untruths about you behind your back, take a deep breath in and out, send light and forgiveness to them, and focus on something else. This is the essence of Deliberate Creation. Going over the situation in your mind countless times is not helpful and doing so will only draw more darkness to you via the Law of Attraction. Writing emails or texts stating your case is not helpful. This will also draw more of this darkness to you. Plus they're not listening and they don't understand you or get you. If they were and they did they wouldn't have said it in the first place.

Learn from your experience. After you've experienced your first painful hit of "hurt" (for some it feels like a drop in the stomach, others like a stab in the heart, others like a wave of nausea, and so on) and that feeling of utter disbelief ("But I thought she was my friend! I trusted him. I believed her.... "), chalk it up to learning and growth and let go. You are now wiser than you were before. Congratulations! You now know things about this person or these people that you didn't know before this experience. And you drew this wisdom to yourself. So find gratitude for your new wisdom. And then think about something else. This all falls under the rubric of Deliberate Creation.

It's all about the power of the focus of your mind. You have a choice. You have the power to focus on something that feels good, even if someone has done or said something that has made you feel bad. Own your power, and use it. This is the practice of Deliberate Creation.

Remember, you will not change other people's opinions or beliefs with your words. No matter how well spoken—how charismatic—how smart—how kind you are, people are wedded to their beliefs for deep-rooted reasons, and mere words from you will not change them.

Instead, simply:

- Live in integrity.

- Send light and love in every situation.

- Don't gossip.

- Speak the truth or say nothing at all.

- Speak with love or say nothing at all.

- Resist the desire to defend yourself.

- Don't take anything personally, no matter how "personal" it seems or feels.

- Teach by your example, by the life you lead.

- Walk your talk.

- Use the power of the focus of your mind to think about things that bring you joy.

- Ask the Universe for help to move thoughts about the painful situation out of your body, mind, and Spirit.

When you follow these simple rules you're in the clear. Anyone can say anything about you and you're immune. Because you know you're clean. You know you're light. You know it has absolutely nothing to do with you. You know it's not personal. You are utilizing Deliberate Creation with grace to create the best life ever. And if it's difficult for you to follow these principles, get on your mat more.

As you live this way, day in and day out, the "he saids/she saids" will slowly but surely fade from your life. Remember, you attract what you put out. So if you give it no energy, it will have to disappear. It is law.

When you follow these simple rules you're in the clear

# Chapter 42
# The Over-the-Top
# First Time Super-Mom

*My job is to relax, appreciate, and enjoy.*

One of my friends just had her first baby. She is forty-four and she keeps saying to me, "Taylor, I had no idea. I had no idea how profound an experience this is." How could she have? No one can until they walk through it.

As I watch her walk the path of "the first-time Super-mom," we both laugh as we think back to me on that path. Man was I over-the-top. I was the over-the-top first-time Super-mom. Most first-time Super-moms are. It's sorta their job. To be neurotic, worrisome, indulgent, obsessive, and, well, just over-the-top.

The thing that makes my friend and me laugh the most is my photo obsession. I still love photos (as evidenced by the number of photos in this book), but this was before the digital camera (my first-born is now fourteen), and so back in the day I took photos, had them developed into multiple hard copies, and put them into piles on my dining room table. Then I'd methodically send them—one pile at a time—to my closest friends and family. I didn't send one or two shots with a thank you note for a gift, I sent envelopes thick with a multitude of shots, and I did so often.

Most first-time Super-moms are. It's sorta their job.

The amount of time, energy (and money) I put into my on-going photo project is staggering and overwhelming to even think about now. And what my friends and family must've thought opening those envelops!

Now I have five kids and I'm psyched if I email a Shutterfly photo album to friends and family once a season. Is the change due to digital cameras, the Internet, and Shutterfly? Partially. But more so, it's due to a lot of yoga and letting go. Letting go of the fear that all first-time Super-moms have. Letting go of the need to capture every single moment on film and then send it to a bunch of people (yikes). Letting go of the need to set up multiple "project stations" in our playroom at 5 am when Madison awoke every morning for the first four years of her life (play dough station, painting station, drawing station, reading station, blocks station...all at 5 am). Letting go of the need to read every parenting book on the market (haven't read one since), buy every hot new developmental toy (haven't bought one since and have given most of hers away since kids really prefer Tupperware to any toy invented by an "expert"), and pack "snacks" like brown rice, tofu, and rice milk for a quick trip to the park.

That's one of the many gifts being a first-time Super-mom gave me—a multitude of lessons in letting go. And letting go is what's necessary to create the best life ever for yourself—whether you're a parent or not. It's about asking for what you want and then letting go and allowing the Universe to create it for you in the best way possible. This means letting go of the illusion of control. If that's challenging for you, just stop thinking about it. Put the wish out there, and then think about other things.

With every manifestation and every miracle you create, you will relax and let go a little more. Armed with the faith that this process works and the three Practices in your toolbox, you will relax and let go even more (just as you do with every child you have), knowing that you are enough without all the fancy toys, multitude of "how to" books, perfect snacks, and photos.

Letting go is what's necessary.

# Chapter 43

# Transitions

"Life is change. Growth is optional. Choose wisely."
- Karen Kaiser Clark

People often ask me what's so great about Prana Power Yoga and why I practice it daily. I feel passionate about this topic, as evidenced by the fact that Philippe and I left the rat race to open our first Prana Power Yoga in 2002, and I've practiced it every single day since, even on the days I've given birth to my children (I practiced the day after my C-section).

The practice is magical. It transforms you in ways you could never anticipate. Sure, it makes you stronger, leaner, more focused, more "in-tune," more patient, more creative, more grounded, and happier; but it also helps you to move with grace and integrity through the transitions of your life.

The transitions between asanas (yoga poses) in a Prana Power Yoga practice are a metaphor for the transitions you experience day-to-day on your path. The point of the practice is to synchronize breath and movement to help the transitions flow more beautifully, organically, and easily. This is why not synchronizing breath and movement in a practice, which sometimes happens when you practice in a gym or health club or with a teacher who isn't experienced, is not really yoga. It's an aerobic workout no doubt, but it's not yoga.

I tell my students, "Your mat is a mirror." As you become more conscious, awake, and aware, you will notice that your practice is a microcosm of you in action day-to-day. Do you rush? Push yourself? Get frustrated? Get impatient? Get angry? Get bored? Strain? Get distracted? Stay focused and calm? Think about the last pose or anticipate the next one? The difficulties in your life will show up on your mat, and your practice on your mat will show up in your life. Immediately. After one practice. I say again and again in class, "You practice it on your mat, and then it shows up in your life." This is why yoga is essential to creating the best life ever. You literally cultivate grace and intention on your mat and then it materializes in your life, helping you to easily utilize Practices two and three concurrently, let go of mental and physical resistance, and therefore create anything you want in your life.

Of course it's OK to show up to your practice with goals like "I want to lose weight" or "I want to look and feel younger." You will get all the benefits to which I am referring without even being aware of what's happening. Because this transformation doesn't come from the mind.

And in time, the "beauty" that you were striving for by practicing (in the form of a more toned and lean body, more beautiful skin, brighter eyes, etc.) will show up in your life. By cultivating "beauty" in your practice through graceful and smooth transitions from pose to pose, this beauty will emanate in your day-to-day life as well.

Transitions are important. As a student wrote to me, "We are in transition more often than not, becoming, not being. Yoga can turn life into a dance. I call it 'living in the flow.'"

# Chapter 44
# Betrayal

*"There is no revenge so complete as forgiveness."*
*- Josh Billings*

One Spring I was going through boxes of old photographs to find a "before" photo for the slide show at The Abundant Prana Conference™. We'd been using "before" and "after" (raw food) photos of other people and decided to take it to another level and use some personal photos as well. Ironically, the very first photo I pulled out "randomly" turned out to be the best photo to use. But Virgo that I am and pregnant Virgo at the time (nesting, nesting, nesting), I found several hours over the next few days to go through six huge boxes of old photos to make sure I found the very best photo for the slide show.

What ensued from those dusty hours walking down memory lane was unexpected. As I sifted through many hundreds, maybe even thousands of photos (I do like my photos), I was surprised by the feelings and epiphanies I was having.

Could alcohol really have played that big of a part of my early twenties? It seemed every party my two post-Brown roommates and I were throwing centered around shots of tequila and kegs. I've always been super social and loved people, and the parties seemed to be nonstop back then in '87, but why the focus on alcohol and the documentation of the inevitable hangover? "This is so not me," I kept thinking as I looked at the outfits I wore (Dear God), the haircut I had, the alcohol I was consuming on a regular basis (once every weekend is a regular basis), but most upsetting, the people with which I was hanging out. Upsetting because I began to be filled with a deep feeling of betrayal.

When I graduated from Brown one of my best friends from college and a mutual friend of ours with whom she'd grown up moved in together in Everett, Massachusetts. We had a great apartment that cost $335 a month each, with three huge bedrooms, two bathrooms, and the kind of dining and living rooms you could really throw a party in (apparently an essential when you're twenty-one).

We were very close, or so I thought, and proclaimed that we'd be friends until Willard Scott from The Today Show announced our birthdays on the air (these were the days when I not only drank tequila shots on the weekends but watched TV as well).

We got along famously—unheard of for three girls. No jealousy, cattiness, competitiveness, or lack of integrity between us. There were the occasional arguments or hurt feelings over two of us spending too much time with our boyfriends (the third roommate didn't have a boyfriend), but we always talked about it and worked it out.

I was however occasionally thrown off by one of my roommates' "ways about the world." She seemed to have no sense of karma—of the fact that everything you do comes back to you. She stole from her employer (in "subtle" ways but nonetheless stealing—taking all of her dry cleaning on business trips and doing it there as an "expense," taking friends who had nothing to do with her job out on her expense account for very expensive eating and drinking extravaganzas, and other

ways that I don't care to recount here), slept with married men who had small children, stole from grocery stores, and bought computers and used them for twenty-nine days, returning them just before the thirty day return policy was up. I loved my friend and chose not to judge but instead to let it go and focus on what I did love about her.

Fast-forward fifteen years. We'd all stood up for each other in our weddings, and now mine was ending. I was heartbroken—going through indescribable pain and grief, and my friends were all there for me. Well, all but two.

One was the wife of a good guy-friend of mine from Brown. My ex-husband and I used to do a lot with her and my Brown guy-friend as a couple when we were married and she dumped me like a hot potato when my "picture perfect marriage and life" wasn't so "picture perfect" anymore. As I looked at the photos, I recalled that she had already "dumped us as a couple" (my ex-husband and me) when my ex-husband got fired from a reputable financial firm. Her phone calls and invitations stopped and when I called her on it she "didn't know what I was talking about."

The other friend who wasn't there for me during my divorce and who, in fact, later refused to come to Philippe and my wedding was, you guessed it, the roomie with a lack of regard for karma. "How could she be judging me?" I asked myself repeatedly. "How could someone who did all those things that were so out of integrity judge me for following my heart and the truth and doing the best thing for my ex-husband and me? How could she not get this? How could she not get me?" And in my darkest and most painful moments, "Why did our friendship end? What did I do wrong?" This question and a deep feeling of betrayal and confusion plagued me on and off for years.

Until the day I was looking through old photos looking for the "before" photo for Abundant Prana. After stirring up all the memories—seeing them in those dusty photo albums from years past—my Spirit came clean, and no surprise where it did so—on my yoga mat at 5:30 am.

This is what came to me, and set me free. The betrayal was not about my friend. It was about me. My betrayal of myself. Of who I know I am. I know that I walk my path with integrity and grace. I know that I'm not perfect by any means but I do my best with breath in each moment. I know that I'm filled with love, light, and forgiveness. I know that I follow my heart and my Spirit—even if it's not the "popular" thing to do at the time. I know that I speak and live truth. I know that I love to inspire and help others. I know that I am love deep down to my core. As are you.

When I asked myself again and again, "What happened? What went wrong? What did I do to lose our friendship?" I was walking down the wrong street. When I went into judgment ("How could she judge me?") I was walking down another street, but the wrong one nonetheless. When I finally—after too many hours of pain and confusion—walked down the path of my Spirit—of love—I felt clarity, and relief.

Sometimes people step out. Sometimes we have something or a lot to do with it, and sometimes we don't. Sometimes it's pure projection. Sometimes it's just time the relationship ends. It has served its purpose in this lifetime and it's over. There are a myriad of reasons that things and relationships change, and the important thing is to stay present and in reality, not in the past. Not in the "but before we . . ." or the "but years ago she said . . .", but instead in, "this moment is as it should be." Otherwise, we are paddling upstream.

How do we know we are paddling upstream? It feels bad. Sometimes really bad. And nothing downstream feels bad. It's easy. It flows beautifully and easily and you feel joy. This is when you know you are practicing Deliberate Creation.

After years of ruminating, I have officially let go of those two friends who dumped me during one of the most challenging times in my life. But without judgment. Without anger. Without resentment. Without guilt. Without regret. I have let them go with love and forgiveness. Because that is the only real way we can let go. "There is no revenge so complete as forgiveness." Otherwise, the anger and the resentment act as magnets, bringing more of that to our lives and us.

But most of all, I have forgiven myself. For questioning my Spirit, for questioning the perfect ways of the Universe, for questioning who I am. Because that's really why I felt betrayed.

# Chapter 45
# Sold Out!

*Everything I want is coming to me fast.*

PHOTO: RAY MUCCI

We were at a matinee the other day with our kiddos and we were literally the only people in the theater. I noticed this and had compassion for the movie theatre owners. I can relate to the preparation involved in "selling out." People go to the movies on Friday or Saturday night, can't get in, and figure it's always like that. But it's not. The movie theater has been open and ready for many a (non-sold-out) show, waiting for that moment. Preparing for that night. And all you see is the sold out moment.

Same thing with a gym or a health club. Ever walk in at a peak time and you can't get on a machine? You probably don't think about it, except that you're annoyed because you have X amount of time to work out and now you have to wait. The reality is that there are many times when those machines aren't taken, when the place is empty and quiet. Empty and quiet, yes, but also preparing, waiting, setting the foundation for "that moment" when it's packed.

Restaurants? Same deal. You walk in on a Friday night at 7 pm, can't get a table, and you're bummed. You're hungry and have a commitment to get to in a few hours and that's all you're aware of. You don't think about the many hours the restaurant was open before you got there, prepping, waiting for your arrival, and laying the foundation to be "sold out."

The metaphor? It's the same with your life. Every step of your path you're prepping and creating the foundation, utilizing the three Practices; waiting for "that moment"—that moment to shine, be happy, of service, respected, loved, recognized, charismatic, inspiring, and all that you can be.

It's different for everyone, but on some level, everyone is waiting for "that moment." You've heard this before with actors—the "overnight successes." Actors laugh when they hear or read this because they've been working their tails off for many years to get to "that moment." There's no such thing as an overnight success. There is always a path leading to that success. But we are only aware of them now. We weren't aware of them during all the years of work and discipline and commitment.

Just like we are only aware of the theater, the restaurant, the gym, and the yoga studio at the moment it's sold out, not taking into account everything it took for it to get to that moment.

# It's the journey, not the destination.

The lesson? It's not the "sold out moment" that really matters. What matters are the many moments strung together to create that moment. It's the journey, not the destination. A happy life is just a string of happy moments. But often people are so busy "trying to get a happy life" that they don't allow the happy moment.

So enjoy the journey and the happy moment and smile when your theater is empty, knowing that soon it will be full and one day, sold out. Just as you've imagined in your mind's eye. It's only a matter of time, energy, and the focus of your mind.

# Chapter 46
# The State of Mind

*"Your thoughts are the primary cause of everything."*
*- Rhonda Byrne*

PHOTO: JENNIFER WELLS

One of my friends has a home in Jamestown, Rhode Island and she and her family like to steal away to it whenever they can. "What do you guys do there?" I asked. "Oh, Taylor, we read, hang out, light a fire, walk to a park, walk to the library, drive into Newport for lunch and a stroll. It's a state of mind," she explained. "Yes, it's a state of mind," I thought to myself.

Everything is, really. Have you ever been on "the vacation from Hell?" I have and it was worse than being home and working fourteen-hour days at a job I didn't love. I was in Florida with my husband at the time, and we had plans to first go to his company's golf get-away, then to Disney World, and end our vacation with a trip to his sister's fiancée's home in Jacksonville, where we'd join their engagement party.

During the golf weekend, the weather was horrendous, the company even worse, and eventually a hurricane just barely missed us. This was before I practiced yoga or knew about Deliberate Creation and The Law of Attraction and my words and thoughts were anything but positive. For the life of me, I couldn't find a positive thing on which to focus. Now I'm so adept at it that I can do so pretty much anywhere and surrounded by anyone.

But I digress.

After the near-hurricane, we packed up our stuff and took off for Disney World. My only recollection of Disney is saying repeatedly, "Why do people like it here? What's the big deal? This place stinks. I want to go home." Not the best way to draw in good-feeling thoughts and experiences. I was in the "Magic Kingdom" and all I could do was criticize and complain.

Next, we drove to Jacksonville for his sister's engagement party. Again, I was miserable. Nothing was right. I was bored, hungry (I didn't like the food they served), and I didn't even think they should be getting married, so why were we celebrating?

We flew out of the "Sunshine State" after those ten miserable days and I couldn't wait to get home. Home to where I could dive back into my job and my routine and ultimately shut down.

At the time, I couldn't see the irony of the situation—that I couldn't wait to stop being on vacation so I could stop being responsible for my feelings, my words, and what I magnetized to myself. All I knew was that it had been the vacation from Hell. Now I understand that I created that Hell. We all create our own Hell and our own joy. It's your choice. In every moment. As it is mine. As you learn to utilize Deliberate Creation with practice, you'll be overjoyed by how you can create your best life ever, especially when concurrently utilizing Practices One and Three.

I am now grateful for that journey, that experience, and that lesson. I will never again experience "the vacation from Hell." Because now I know that it's all a state of mind.

# Chapter 47
# Let's Begin Again

It was only a shift in perspective, as all miracles are.

PHOTO: KELLY LORENZ

It was Monday morning, 8:27 am. Madison's school began at 8:35 am and Sagey's at 8:30 am. I was teaching yoga at Prana Power Yoga Newton at 9 am. My intention was to leave the house at 8:10 am, drop Madison at school at 8:20 am, Sagey at preschool at 8:30 am, and then drive to the studio with plenty of time to begin class at 9 am sharp. But we were just getting in the car. How did this happen? Where did the time go?

I was up at 4 am, did two hours of work on the computer before the baby woke up, nursed the baby (Phoenix, now age five, a baby at the time), changed his diaper, got him dressed, got the kids' breakfast, helped them get dressed, brush their teeth, take their vitamins, and get their lunches and backpacks ready to go. Still on track to leave.

Then Madison needed something upstairs, Sagey wanted her hair put up in her pink and purple ribbon, the baby needed another diaper change and wanted to practice walking with me.

Still on track to be on time. But now Sagey needed to go potty and needed help wiping and Madison needed a check for hot lunches which she'd forgotten to ask me about the night before.

Now finally getting in the car—still going to make it—but not exactly as I'd "planned," and... no car seat for Sagey. We'd taken it out the day before for a play date at a friend's house and hadn't put it back in the car.

The positive energy with which we began our day, with lit candles, positive affirmations, yoga, and homemade Brazil nut milk, had shifted dramatically and everyone's vibration was low. We were vibrating at "stressed out," a vibration many Super-moms in Newton, Massachusetts experience between 8:22 and 8:35am on school days.

Car seat in, engine on, and backing out of the driveway, I had a choice: keep vibrating at this level and suffer, or stop, and begin again.

I chose the latter, thanks to years of yoga and Deliberate Creation. "Let's begin again," I said to my kids.

And we did, just like that, chatting joyfully about the day and our outing planned after school, with only a vestige of the negative energy still present that was only seconds before creating our mood, our moment, and our future. And it was only a shift in perspective. As all miracles are.

"Let's begin again," I said to my kids. And we did, just like that, chatting joyfully.

# Chapter 48
# A Night In The ER

Turn your attention to the positive aspects of others.

PHOTO: KELLY LORENZ

"Mommy, I'm scared."

That's all I needed to hear. I was immediately on the phone to our pediatrician, who, thank goodness, was on call that night. My (then) ten-year-old Madison was not a drama queen and she'd been sick for four days, and it was getting worse. Her tummy was in a lot of sharp pain and I was concerned about her appendix. As I had intuited, the doc said, "Go to the ER—now."

My ex-husband took Madison into the hospital since she was sleeping at his house that night. I got Phoenix (then one-year-old) and Sagey (then three-years-old) down to sleep, and then met them at the ER. Four hours later, we were called into a room.

Four hours in the waiting room of the ER with your ex-husband and a very sick child. "What could be worse?" you ask.

Actually, it was beautiful. The entire experience. My ex-husband and I got along well as we waited, chatting and laughing a lot as our ten-year-old basked in the glow of watching her parents hang out together for more than the usual few minutes during pickups and drop-offs. So much so that her tummy hurt less.

Many years ago, I prayed day in and day out for a "mutual, loving, and gentle resolution" between my ex-husband and me. I had faith, prayed, visualized, and believed. I also practiced a lot of yoga.

Now many years later, after teaching a yoga class that very morning about "the beauty, importance, and healing power of laughter," the Universe was delivering that laughter to me—in the emergency room with my ex-husband and our sick daughter. Yet another reminder to remain completely open to how the Universe delivers your wish—to whatever package it arrives in.

At about 1:30 am we all trudged out of the ER, prognosis: positive. Both for a healthy child with some rest and TLC (no appendicitis) and a mutual, loving, and gentle relationship between her Mom and Dad.

# Chapter 49
# Motivation

"I think self-awareness is probably the most important
thing towards being a champion."
- Billie Jean King

PHOTO: TAYLOR WELLS

A wise teacher once told me that motivation is the ability to force yourself to act, whereas inspiration is the impulse to act.

To be "inspired" means, quite literally, to be "in Spirit," or "with your Spirit." So when you are inspired, you are "in the flow." Life flows through you and for you. Things don't happen "to" you, things happen "for" you.

I used to live my life fueled mostly by motivation, and I'm here to tell ya that that ain't no way to live.

You'd never have known by looking at my resume.´ I had "it all." The degrees, the accolades, the Ivy Leagues—you name it. It was "mine." What was missing? Joy. Love. Grace. Freedom. Inspiration.

My mind was checking everything off my list, one by one, as my body ached with pain from this and that ailment and illness and my Spirit suffocated. Even my relationship with my husband at the time reflected this stagnant energy.

Then one day it all came to a screeching halt. What opened my eyes? My yoga practice. As I breathed in and breathed out and moved through the poses passed down for over five centuries, I began to let go and my Spirit began to speak. And once it began, there was no stoppin' it.

Motivation is the ability to force your- self to act, whereas inspiration is the impulse to act.

Things began to fall away naturally. Toxic things that didn't belong in my life and weren't serving me "got off the bus." Friendships that had long since ended moved on and new friendships brimming with joy, love, connection, and promise began. Excess clothes found their way into bags to be given to charity. Various "things" in my home that weren't me and cluttered my mind and my life found other homes. Even my body changed—effortlessly and quickly.

With every single practice, I became lighter—body and mind—and began to feel joy and peace. Peace! I had had no idea what this was at the time. No idea.

Years before when my therapist asked me to visualize a place that felt "peaceful," it caused me even more anxiety as I attempted to figure out what she "wanted" me to say. I had no idea what peace was or what it even looked or felt like. Let's just say peace wasn't my every step, or any of my steps. I was a "doer," and do I did. But peace and joy weren't part of the package.

So yes, I was "motivated," but motivated by fear. Fear of not being enough. Fear of the anxiety that would pervade me if I weren't always doing something, achieving something, moving "forward"—whatever that meant.

But now, after committing to a regular yoga practice, I have found a life of inspiration and I have found peace. A true and deep inner peace. This is a whole different way to live, thank the

Universe. Being inspired means following your intuition—what feels right? Listening to what your heart wants to do right now, instead of being glued to a "to do" list.

This takes courage. Your yoga practice will give you the courage. By breathing away fear on your mat regularly, you open up and create the space for anything that you want. You create the potential—your pure potential—which has always been there. It's just been hiding behind fear.

"Motivation," admired by so many, is actually fueled by fear. So yes, you'll "go far" fueled by motivation; but only so far, and there will be relatively little joy and peace, if any.

Inspiration, on the other hand, is the gateway to pure potential. You can literally be, do, and have anything that you want. If you follow your Spirit, follow your heart, and believe, utilizing the three Practices.

So when people ask me, "How do you do all that you do with five kids?" I tell them that it's easy. As long as I do my daily yoga practice and live by these words: Only do what your Spirit loves and cultivate true freedom in every aspect of your life (Practices two and three).

Because when you only do what your Spirit loves, you are inspired (in-Spirit), and your main vibration is joy and appreciation. From there, anything and everything is possible. The "pressure of time" slips away and everything lines up easily. You are always at the right place at the right time meeting the right people and being offered the best opportunities. Everything feels and is easy.

Why? Because it's all about your energy and vibration. What you put out comes back to you—always. This is The Law of Attraction.

# Chapter 50
# The Proposal(s)

In everything look beneath
the surface to see what's really there.

When I was twenty-five my boyfriend of seven years proposed to me on one knee while I brushed my teeth sitting on the toilet (seat closed) wearing my PJ's. I was so thrilled that he asked (after seven years together and a very painful breakup after six years which I initiated), that the "how it happened" didn't faze me, nor did the fact that he didn't have a ring. To be honest, I didn't really notice. I'd never been into appearances and so it just didn't matter to me. It was only when I was asked repeatedly, "Oh my God! How did he propose? What does the ring look like? Where is it?" that I began to feel uncomfortable. When I recounted the proposal, by request, people's faces were, uh, slightly horrified.

Fast-forward fourteen years. My first husband and I had divorced (and remained friends) and I was talking to the new love of my life—my soul mate—on the phone. Not about anything particular or anything very deep, just chatting. He was telling me about a wedding he'd gone to and how he was talking to a friend of his who commented that he and I "were really already married." I laughed happily and Philippe followed with, "Well, do you wanna then?"

"Wanna what?" I asked, completely clueless. "Get married?" he asked.

"Sure!" I blurted out, without skipping a beat. My Spirit spoke for me before my mind could step in and perhaps allow a slight pause for good measure.

And that was it. We were engaged. Proposal done—on the phone—and again, without a ring. (I actually specifically didn't want a ring this time, and had made this very clear to Philippe—you'll read more about this in the next chapter.)

When Philippe told his mother how he'd proposed to me she was horrified and said, "Vell, she must be cwazy about you to have accepted a proposal like that!" (That's my attempt at capturing her Swiss German accent on paper).

It occurred to me later that I indeed manifested both of these, err, rather "unconventional" proposals, as I've manifested everything else in my life. But why?

Then it came to me. I manifested them because they are indicative of my beliefs—that it's not what's on the "outside" that counts. It's not the "flashy-ness" or "romance" of a proposal that counts, but the integrity and true and deep love in it.

I know a guy who engineered a super fancy, super romantic proposal. He flew his girlfriend to Chicago for a Bears football game (her favorite football team) and had a plane fly overhead asking her to marry him. They lasted about two years. He cheated on her repeatedly (even before the wedding) and she found out.

I know another guy who had a reallllly expensive ring put in a fancy ice cream dish at an expensive restaurant in Paris, where they'd flown for "fun" and "romance." No, she didn't bite it (the ring in

It's what's underneath that counts.

her ice cream), but their marriage did—after nine months.

"But wait," you object. "Your first marriage (that involved the proposal on a toilet) bit it too, Super-mom. It was a failure." But I disagree. My first marriage was not a failure. It was destined to be. When I met Andy the first day of orientation week at Brown I told all of my friends, "That's the man I'm going to marry," and I don't regret one moment of our time together. We grew up together, loved each other, evolved a lot, and eventually grew apart. But not before creating the most magical daughter I could have ever wanted. A daughter who knows in her heart when she watches her dad and I interact, that we will always love each other, even though we can't live together anymore.

The moral of my story? It's not that really cool and romantic proposals are bad. That would be so sour grapes. It's that in life (not just proposals), it's what's underneath that counts. So in everything—a proposal, a compliment, an insult, a question, a job offer, a proposition, an email—look beneath the surface to see what's really there.

The more yoga you practice, the more this is simply second nature. And that's why the yogic path is almost always clear and joyful. If you are present enough to listen from within.

# Chapter 51
# The Ring

*"It's all about fun."*
*- Roger Lewis*

When Philippe and I got married, I didn't want an engagement ring. I actually didn't want to wear a ring at all and here's why. When I married my first love at age twenty-five he was very into the ring and jewelry thang, and I went along with it—even though my Spirit didn't feel quite right with the whole focus on material things. It meant a lot to him and he meant a lot to me so I didn't speak my truth at the time. That would change with time and lots of yoga.

So back in the day, I had an engagement ring (given to me a few months after he asked me to marry him) and a wedding ring, and then Andy continued to buy me beautiful jewelry throughout our ten-year marriage. It was his thing, like it was his father's thing before him. But it never quite fit. Energetically. I felt oddly confined by the jewelry—claustrophobic. A harbinger of things to come.... They were given from love, so I was grateful, and let the energetics of it go.

When I married Philippe he wore a ring from day one of our Spiritual Union and loved it. I on the other hand felt that I didn't want to be "branded" and feel like I "had" to wear this loaded symbol that said this or that about me and stood for so many different things to so many people. I also wanted to support the many single people out there who feel triggered by rings and such and it just felt right for me to be ring-less. Philippe was down with this, so that's how it went down.

In comes Kelly, our beloved photographer, student, and friend, who tells me all about the diamond mines and what they're really about. About the child slavery. About the bad stuff that goes down in the name of these "gemstones" that we've all been brainwashed are "the real deal." It occurred to me that this is part of the reason diamonds always felt uncomfortable to me—my Spirit felt this energy.

I read up on the whole diamond industry debacle and was sad about what has happened and is happening, and vowed to personally boycott diamonds. This was and is a very personal choice. I didn't and don't feel offended if other people wear diamonds, and chances are they don't know about the whole situation or perhaps they wouldn't be wearing them.

Then one crisp autumn day we were strolling down Saint Mark's Place in the East Village of Manhattan after teaching at our Prana Power Yoga studio in Union Square and I came upon the most beautiful and sparkly thing ever. (I never said I didn't like sparkles.) In fact, it's all about sparkles and glitter for this Super-mom and her kids. It was a big 'ole cubic zirconia "engagement" ring (some sort of "cut" that is classic, although I'm not well-versed in that nomenclature so I couldn't tell you which one), with a matching "wedding" band to boot. These rings were so sparkly that they drew me right in. "I love these!" I exclaimed to Philippe. "Get em!" he said with a smile.

So thirty-two dollars later, I was wearing the most sparkly and happy rings ever. And loving them. Now these rings felt right. These rings felt fun. These rings felt sparkly. And oh-so-ironically, I felt (and still do) that these rings are prettier and more sparkly than any diamond I've ever seen. I was at peace with these rings, even on my "ring finger."

Fast-forward one week. We were back in the state of Massachusetts and I experienced something for which I was unprepared. Seeing me donning my new sparkly gems, my yoga students were taken aback. They'd be talking to me and their eyes would wander to my rings and they'd stop talking and lose their train of thought. Only a few had the courage to say, "Oh my God! What are those?" (I told you these rings were big and sparkly.) I was at a loss for words (unusual for me). There was so much history—so much to say, to explain. Did I start way back at age twenty-five? At the discovery of the diamond child slave situation? At my feminist views on ring wearing that had changed oh-so-abruptly that fall day on Saint Marks Place?

It was so surprising and bizarre to me how differently people treated me while I was wearing the rings. I guess they thought I was wearing a fifty thousand dollar diamond (if it were a diamond, it would be at least fifty thousand dollars—this ring is big), and somehow this "changed" me? I was confused.

I began thinking about how big diamond companies have truly brainwashed a whole country. I personally like how cubic zirconias look better than diamonds; yet, a cubic zirconia is considered "fake." Fake compared to what? Who decided that diamonds are "precious?" Are they precious because so many children's and people's lives are ruined while mining them? Are they precious because they've made a few big diamond companies very wealthy? (Not that there's anything wrong with abundance). Is that what makes a stone "precious" and "of high value?" I've always had my different ways of looking at the world, so it's no surprise that herein lays another way that I beg to differ.

As I wear my rings now (when I feel like it, usually just from time to time for fun), I'm proud to know that I wear them for my own reasons, and not because a huge company spent a lot of money brainwashing a country that one thing was prettier than another, at the cost of treating both children and adults inconsiderately at best. I wear them because they are sparkly and remind me of the light of the Universe, the light that shines within each one of us. I wear them because they remind me of that chilly Autumn day in the East Village of Manhattan, when my beloved spiritual partner said without hesitation, "Get em!" because he saw the sparkle in my eye, reflected in my new purchase on my ring finger. I wear them because they're fun. And it's all about fun.

Also, I would personally rather put thirty-two dollars toward my sparkly rings and put the fifty thousand dollars toward opening another Prana Power Yoga Studio. Not that there's anything wrong with fifty thousand dollar rings, you out there who don 'em. The key is that it needs to feel right and great for you.

On a similar note, for all of you diamond wearers out there, rock on! I was wearing a diamond back in the day (before I knew what I know now) and I don't judge anyone or anything. Period. That's my yoga. If you love it and it makes you happy, that's what matters. Do, write, wear, eat, have, and be what you love and don't worry or even think about "the peanut gallery." When you are following your heart you are always on the right path. Always. No matter what you do, say, and are, you can't please everyone, so listen to your heart and watch everything fall into place easily, as it should.

# Chapter 52
# The Children's Museum

"Your children need your presence
more than your presents."
- Jesse Jackson

PHOTO: KELLY LORENZ

When I was twenty-six weeks pregnant with our twins we went on a "staycation." We drove all of seven minutes from Newton, Massachusetts to downtown Boston and stayed in a hotel in the city, swimming in their pool, walking around the city, checking out the mall in which the hotel resides, browsing bookstores on Newbury Street, eating out, watching a (free) movie in the room, etc. It's a vacation without the travel! Since I was twenty-six weeks pregnant with twins my body and intuition wouldn't allow me to travel further than ten minutes away. My body thought I was about to go into labor since at twenty-six weeks with two babies in my belly I felt like I did when I was full-term and about to deliver my first three (singleton) children.

So off we went to the Westin Copley with very little in hand, to enjoy each other and a little "time away." My kids love to swim and so do Philippe and I. I feel weightless while swimming, which is always nice when you're pregnant. We spent hours in the pool as our daily and nightly routines went out the window. We swam late, jacuzzied, showered, and then hit the streets and the restaurants at about nine pm (my kids usually go to sleep at seven on a "good night.")

By the time we'd walked and eaten and walked again, it was super late. "We're on a staycation!" I proclaimed. "Let's watch a movie!" Watch we did—till about midnight and one at a time, our kids fell off to sleep in the bed next to ours.

Thankfully, our kids slept late the next morning and when they awoke off we went to take another dip in the pool. We swam and played and had a blast, and as the clock ticked on, started to make

"We're on a staycation!"

plans for the rest of the day. I'm a yogi and like to live in the moment and go with the flow, so making plans is not my thang; however, my kids were all excited to talk about what they wanted to do, so plan we did. The bookstore! Newbury Street! The mall! The ice cream store! On and on the list went.

We ventured out and did our best to hit all the spots my kids had their hearts set on. Then with about two hours until we needed to be back home for a yoga class, my kids declared that they wanted to go to the Children's Museum. We were headed to the ice cream store and Philippe and I explained that we couldn't do both so they would need to make a choice since we still needed to walk back to the hotel, pack up, check out, and be home in two hours. "ICE CREAM STORE!" they all exclaimed. No clarity needed there.

The girls enjoyed Oreo and peanut butter ice cream with sprinkles while Phoenix, 100% raw vegan at the time, enjoyed the "tea cup" chair and couldn't care less about the ice cream. Then we all walked back to the hotel.

As we were packing up, I checked the time and noticed that if we booked we could stop at The Children's Museum for a quick visit on our way home. I explained this to the kids and they were ecstatic.

We checked out, drove to the Museum, and Philippe took them in while I sat parked in an illegal parking spot since the parking at the Children's Museum is dicey. We explained to the kids clearly that they could do three things—that this would be a quick visit. Yes, yes, they understood.

Thirty minutes later as they piled back into the car I fielded all the discontent. "Papa! Why did we have to go?" They asked Philippe. "We only got to do three thingggggggsssssss!" they continued.

"Guys," I reminded them, "You chose the ice cream store over the Children's Museum and the fact that you got to go to the museum at all was a huge gift!" "But I reallllly wanted to do the space walk, Mommy!" they whined. "Kids, you knew you got to do three things, and three things you did!" I said positively yet firmly.

On and on it went. I was astounded. I reminded them how blessed they were to have stayed in a hotel in Boston, gone swimming (twice!), jacuzzied, walked through the city and the mall, eaten dinner out, gone to bookstores, gotten ice cream, and now gone to the Children's Museum! "Where's the gratitude?" I asked in disbelief. "If we had 'just' gone for ice cream, you would've been ecstatic, and now you're complaining after having done fifteen billion things!"

Then I remembered one of the many lessons I've learned since becoming a Super-mom fourteen years ago. Kids are young enough to remember that asking and having it given is their birthright. They haven't yet learned to doubt, wonder and fear. They want something and they expect to get it. And this is actually the basis—the genius—behind manifesting—behind Deliberate Creation.

Now you can look at this as being "spoiled" or you can look at it as them owning their birthright—being in their power. I'm a big fan of choosing the positive thought, so I chose the latter. Instead of getting angry, I laughed at the irony that children are often mesmerized and entertained by the simplest things (a butterfly, a bumble bee, a wide open field of grass, bubble wrap) but at the same time, after twenty-four hours of nonstop fun activities, they'll complain about "only" getting to do three things at the Children's Museum. And want MORE. They will always push for more. Always.

Their little Spirits know that's how The Universe and The Law of Attraction work.

As a Super-mom, what I've learned is that I can get annoyed or angry and see them as ungrateful and "spoiled," or I can learn from their unwavering belief in their right to have that which they ask for. Their steadfastness in always wanting and asking for more, because their little Spirits know that's how The Universe and The Law of Attraction work—if we believe and have little or no resistance.

I choose to learn from my kids as my teachers and let go of the illusion of control, while concurrently teaching them about gratitude for what they do have. It's a balance, just like everything else.

# Chapter 53
# Full and Starving

*"What you do speaks so loud that
I cannot hear you speak."
- Ralph Waldo Emerson*

When I was little, my legs were just my legs. I never thought about them. My arms were just my arms. They helped me hit a tennis ball, to win a match. I never thought about whether they were thin, toned, whether they fit into the "right" size of clothing.

I never thought about food either. Except for the habitual question, "Mom, what's for dinner?" food wouldn't cross my mind, unless the Good Humor ice cream truck was driving down my street in Lake Bluff, Illinois.

How is it that our culture has become so obsessed with food and so hyper-aware of our physical bodies? Since our body is really just "the home of our Spirit," why do we constantly obsess about it and what we put into it? And how can we stop?

Here's my take. People aren't paying attention or listening to what their bodies are telling them as they eat because many have lost their ability to judge real hunger and real cravings and to feed them. This coupled with the fact that many of us learned at some point on our journey that some foods are "bad" and others "good," is a recipe for not cultivating and utilizing complete freedom with food.

People are full—and starving. Starving for balance, guidance, peace, love, joy, and light. They wanna be healthy and wanna feel good, but they're lost. People, like you, want the best life ever—that's why you're reading this book.

Where did it all go wrong? I can't pinpoint where or how it all went wrong, but I can say how it shifted or "went right" for me: the three Practices. I utilize them daily and the mystery is solved. Life is good—the best ever!

I have a ton of energy, feel happy pretty much all of the time (except when I briefly experience contrast, note what I do want, then ignore the contrast—what I don't want—and focus on something else, utilizing Deliberate Creation), need less sleep, and have more clarity, focus, and patience. The three Practices not only create the best life ever for me but also make me a better parent, wife, teacher, friend, writer, and person. I am better able to be of service to my family and friends, my yoga students and community, my Prana Power Yoga teaching staff, the person on the street who needs help, and the world.

People ask me, "Taylor, is it really that simple?"

Yes, it is. But you need to utilize the three Practices for it to work. Now is the perfect time to start.

# Chapter 54
# The Weather

What I think, talk about, and feel and what
comes back to me is always a vibrational match.

PHOTO: TAYLOR WELLS

It's cold, snowy, and icy outside. Really cold (7 degrees Fahrenheit), snowy, and icy. We live in New England and it's the last day of January. Of course it's really cold, snowy, and icy! Yet, I hear them all the time—complaints about the weather. Haven't people come to expect that this weather will come every year at this time? And what does it have to do with anything? So you walk a little slower, you bundle up, you make sure your hair is dry before you hit the cold temps.

To me, the reliance on weather being perfect for you to feel good is a metaphor for "letting 'the outside' determine your 'inside' life." How you and I feel on the inside has nothing to do with external events. It has to do with how we process them internally. This is key when utilizing Deliberate Creation, and practicing yoga and free and balanced eating will help you to do so. They all work and flow together seamlessly.

You know this. You've seen examples of people living in this higher flow and those who are not, even though their life may be filled with many gifts. I'm referring to the person who "has it all" but

# Utilizing the Law of Attraction, you create the best life ever.

complains about not being happy and the guy who picks you up in a cab in NYC who has eight hungry mouths to feed and an apartment the size of a closet but is in the best mood ever all the time. It's not what's on "the outside" but what's on "the inside" that matters.

"But Taylor, how do I make what's on the 'inside' shiny and bright so my world reflects that?" you ask. Simple. Deliberate Creation in concert with your yoga practice and free and balanced eating. Utilizing The Law Of Attraction, you create the best life ever by thinking good thoughts. It doesn't matter what

they're about, just think them. If you need to think about a sunset in the Caribbean that you have only seen in a magazine, do it. If you need to imagine your dream soul mate who hasn't appeared yet, do it. If you need to think about a basketball game where you score the winning point (even if this has never happened), do it. Whatever floats your boat—brings you joy—that is what your thoughts should focus on. This is the essence of manifesting. This is the essence of practicing Deliberate Creation.

The irony is that as you do so, the "outer" events in your life will reflect back the joy you've been experiencing just by imagining things in your mind (whether they've actually ever happened or not).

Try it! What do you have to lose? Besides some negative thoughts and experiences.

# Chapter 55
# The Seat Belt

When you're in perfect vibrational harmony your
body produces whatever it needs to be in balance.

We got a minivan. I ate my words, and they tasted good. I was the one who made fun of people with minivans (pre-yoga), and swore I would never-ever-not-ever drive one.

Our third baby was due shortly and we did the math. Pickups from school and play dates with many friends in tow were not going to work with our new baby in our SUV.

The coolest part of the minivan? It's challenging to choose one, so I'll say two: the space (I could walk to the back and nurse my third baby while we were driving to teach at Prana NYC—while he was still strapped in! Being flexible from yoga is good for many day-to-day things) and the automatic opening doors.

The most annoying part? Again, I'll choose two things: how bad it is for our environment (gasp) and the "seat belt beep."

"What," you ask, "Is the seat belt beep?" It's an ear-piercing beep that's relentless—until you actually buckle up. "Beep beep beep," it's telling you, "Buckle up or pay the consequences." "Beep, beep, beep," it's warning, "You've read the statistics about seatbelts, so just do it. Beep, beep, beep," it's begging you, "C'mon buddy, it takes a second and will save your life." And it keeps on beeping and beeping and beeping...until, it stops.

I do wear my seatbelt, so how would I know about this? I know because a few times I've been zipping up my fleece or putting a bag in the back seat or handing a hungry mini traveler a snack, and although my intention is to buckle up and I am planning to do so in a sec, the beeping device doesn't know this.

So one day when the beeping just stopped after a while it occurred to me that it was as if it was saying, "Fine, hurt yourself. I tried to warn you—to remind you—but you just aren't listening."

And so it is with our emotions and our health. We get the warning signals—the beeping if you will—the headache, stress, too little sleep, not enough R & R, not enough yoga, the cold, the flu, the irritability, the anger, the fear (often caused by not speaking your truth, not following your heart, not enjoying any down time, not eating well, not sleeping well)...but are we listening?

Are we listening to the signals or medicating them with "more?" More food, more stuff, more exercise, more alcohol, more drugs. Isn't it easier and more enjoyable to just buckle up before the beeping begins?

But how do we do that? Easy. Practice yoga often, eat what you love in moderation and without restriction, sleep well, listen to your heart, speak your truth, be kind, and talk and think about your hopes and dreams and things that make you happy. This is my Rx for avoiding the drama all together—both the beeping and the subsequent disasters.

# Chapter 56
# The 100 Days

Resistance takes a toll on the number
of great things you allow.

And so it happened. The Shift. I was about 6 months pregnant with my twin boys and it hit me, "I have only one-hundred days left of my twin pregnancy, I should relish every moment instead of impatiently counting the days till I deliver." From tolerating to enjoying. In an instant.

From annoyance at the increasing difficulty of sleeping, tying my shoes, and just moving through the world, to the awe of my belly burgeoning beyond anything anyone could imagine was possible. As transformational moments often are, it was like a flash—a moment when everything became clear.

I remembered how once the baby (babies in my case) is born, the post-partum Super-mom is all but forgotten. If you've ever had a baby you know that at that point, it's all about the baby. As well it should be. But I've heard some Super-moms talk about how abrupt the transition is. When you're pregnant people are all about, "How are you feeling?" "Oh let me open the door for you." "Please lemme carry that for you." "May I get you something to eat or drink?" "Wow, when are you due?"

Then you give birth and it's all about the baby, and the Super-mom who just gave birth is an after thought. Plus in the fog of nursing, diapers, sleep deprivation, caring for your other children, and just keeping up with the day-to-day of life, Super-mom can get lost in the shuffle.

So it hit me—I'd better enjoy this while I can. It really is just a state of mind. This is the essence of Deliberate Creation.

So I learned to smile and find gratitude and joy when I donned a bikini to swim a half-mile daily at the Y and people asked me repeatedly if I was due tomorrow. My belly looked like it did when I delivered my singletons and so of course they asked that.

# Letting go of the illusion of control and allowing the wisdom of my babies to reign.

I surrendered to the sometimes sleepless nights, sleeping when I could sleep, letting go of the illusion of control and allowing the wisdom of my babies to reign. I said, "Yes, please" with a smile and gratitude when someone offered me kindness or some help with anything. I enjoyed each moment of the miracle of creating two lives in my belly and tuned into the excitement and wonder of meeting my two baby sons.

# Chapter 57
# The Fast
# Moving Stream

"It's always easier to fight for your principles
than to live up to them."
- Adlai Stevenson

At this point in my life I know a lot about The Law Of Attraction and Deliberate Creation. So you could say I "know better" than to focus on something that I don't want. I know viscerally that whatever I focus on—wanted or unwanted—I am creating. But sometimes "that thing" happens which magnetizes your attention again and again despite your best and "most awakened and aware" efforts.

This "thing" happened "to me" one Friday night when I was twenty-six weeks pregnant with our twin boys. I put "to me" in quotations because I take full responsibility for attracting every single thing I have attracted into my life—wanted and unwanted. This is key when practicing Deliberate Creation. It's easy and fun to take responsibility for all the good, fun, and happy stuff. But the Law of Attraction don't choose and discriminate. It delivers what you puttin' out, 24/7. No exceptions.

It was the eve of our second Prana Power Yoga Teacher Training 2010 weekend. Philippe and I were getting our kids down and then planning to prepare for the following fun and adventure-filled day with our fifty wonderful Prana teacher trainees.

I was on the phone with one of our Prana Power Yoga teachers and bam! My heart skipped a beat as she dropped a "betrayal bomb" on me so intense that I felt like I was going to throw up. The details don't matter. What matters is the energy with which I received this information and why I had attracted it into my life. I knew that the reason would become clear and relatively quickly because I would ask my higher self, "What's the lesson here? What do I need to learn? What do I need to do differently?" and the answer would come. But it hurt. Deep down in my heart.

As I laid with my children in their bed that night and waited for them to drift softly off to sleep I kept watching them, finding gratitude for all they are and all the joy, adventure, fun, and wisdom they bring me every single moment of every single day. As they closed their eyes peacefully and breathed in and breathed out, I focused on how beautiful and perfect they are. I was attempting to distract myself from the "yoga drama" at hand and it worked for a minute, until the thoughts returned.

Once they were sleeping soundly I tiptoed out of their room and down to Philippe, the one person who would really "get" what I was feeling, as he too was feeling what I was feeling, or his version of it.

We talked about what had happened, what was happening, and how it felt, and I said to him, "I know I shouldn't focus on this. I know I need to let it go. But I'm giving myself tonight to be hurt and angry. Just the next two hours before I go to sleep to 'kvetch,' and I promise you and my higher self that come morning time, I will have let it go."

So I did. I allowed myself to focus on all that dark energy. To toss it over in my suffering mind. A pleasant one hundred and twenty minutes it wasn't. I awoke a few times in the night and negative thoughts about the drama filled my mind immediately. Of course they did—I'd gone to sleep thinkin' about it. I felt misunderstood. I felt hurt and angry. I felt disrespected. I felt that a few people had lost their sense of gratitude and were acting out of integrity. On and on those thoughts went.

True to my intention and my word when I awoke the next morning to the sun shining through the window onto my face, I had let it all go. I didn't think about it anymore. I focused on anything and everything but. This is Deliberate Creation in action.

While I was on my mat that morning Philippe called one of the people involved in the drama and set some important "no-brainer" boundaries that anyone who's ever been in a leadership position would totally get, and although I heard bits and pieces of the muffled conversation as I practiced, it affected me not. I was back in the Vortex (the joyful place where anything and everything is possible). I was practicing yoga and Deliberate Creation concurrently so it didn't matter to me if the person on the other end of the phone "got it" or not. I knew that we were in integrity and being the leaders that our Spirits had designated us to be. You can only be a leader to those who are in the same vibrational place as you. If you are residing in the Vortex and the person you're talking with is not, very little real communication will take place. You've experienced this. You talk and talk, but the person don't hear a word you say. Man, is that exhausting.

So, off we went to teach Prana Power Yoga and much more to fifty lovely and bright Teacher Training students and all flowed as it should.

The following morning I woke up in a great space, hopped on my mat to practice before taking our kids swimming at the Y, and bam! They were back. "Those" thoughts. They weren't nearly as deleterious as those I experienced on Friday night but they still felt bad. They were the flavor of: "How can she think that? How could she say that? How can she be so ungrateful and disrespectful?" And so on. This type of thinking is never a good thing. This is not practicing Deliberate Creation but instead an example of contrast.

Because of my fervent and dedicated practice of Deliberate Creation, utilizing The Law of Attraction to the best of my ability, my life usually flows

I was back in the Vortex (the joyful place where anything and everything is possible.)

beautifully and easily. People show up with a smile. I'm mostly always at the right place at the right time meeting the right people and being offered the best opportunities to make it the best day ever every day. But not so on that day. I had "made my bed" earlier with "those" thoughts and "that" negative energy and The Universe was about to deliver, as it always does.

After my practice my kids and I scooted to the women's changing room at the Y where I got my little ones in their suits, caps, and goggles in record time. I was gonna swim a half mile first while Philippe played with the kids in the water and then he'd swim laps while I splashed around with them. Then Philippe would pick up a delicious raw vegan lunch at our Prana Restaurant (we were still raw vegan and still owned the restaurant at the time) while I showered the kids and took them oh-so-briefly into the sauna and steam room. We had a play date scheduled at home at two so we had just the right amount of time if everything flowed.

But it didn't. The three kids and I waited for Philippe at the pool for fifteen minutes. "What is he doing?" we kept wondering, annoyed, since my husband is about as low maintenance as they come and changes in a millisecond. He finally showed up and I scooted up to the cardio area where I planned to walk for ten minutes before my swim, on order from my chiropractor who said I needed to walk ten minutes a day to incorporate the integral work she was doing. I hopped onto the treadmill, walked for a minute or so and then mistakenly yanked out the emergency stop cord and SLAM! The treadmill stopped abruptly. Thank the Universe I have a good sense of balance so my twins and I didn't wipe out. I was trying to figure out how to start it up again when the woman next to me said, "Hi Taylor! Are you trying to plug in your iPod?" It was a (former) student of Prana Power Yoga who no longer practices at Prana because she declared that a teacher at another studio was "cute" and so she was "done with Prana Power Yoga" (yes, she really did say this to me). I smiled, said no thank you, and found another treadmill.

Ten minutes later I stopped at the pool to check on the kids and Philippe before changing into my suit, and there were my three little angels, sitting on the side of the pool with their toes dangling in, looking forlorn as Philippe swam the butterfly as only he can.

Before I got to my kids, the lifeguard stopped me and sweetly explained that it wasn't family swim yet—not for two more hours—and although he wanted to, he couldn't let my kids swim because he would get in trouble. If he let my kids swim then all the other kids would want to swim during non-family swim. I smiled as I said, "No worries," and meant it.

I gathered up my kids and told Philippe we were going to check out the kids' playroom that we'd heard about. I told my kids I was sorry about the swimming, that I'd read an old schedule and it wasn't family swim yet, and that we'd make the most of this and have a different and fun adventure (Deliberate Creation).

We stopped at the front desk to get directions to the playroom and the woman said it was closed. That was quite simply "it" for me, and I lost it, Super-mom style. "No family swim and no playroom on a Sunday early afternoon? How is this a family Y?" I asked incredulously. The poor woman just looked at me. What could she say? I grabbed my three-year-old's hand and stomped away, with an oh-so-bitchy energy that's so not me.

> We found an alternative fun activity—the kids' exercise room.

We found an alternative fun activity—the kids' exercise room—and my kids were in heaven. I got them situated and put Madison (age thirteen at the time) in charge, and went over with her several times the importance of always watching her three and five-year-old siblings. She got it and they were the only ones in the room, so I felt comfortable leaving them briefly in the care of their big sis.

I scooted to the changing room, donned my suit, cap, and goggles, and slipped into the pool and the meditative flow of swimming a half-mile. Weightless in the pool, I felt reborn and recharged and cleared my energy (this was my "yoga" in that moment). As thoughts came in about the yoga drama I did my best to move them out and focus on anything else (Deliberate Creation).

I finished swimming, smiled at the lifeguard, and headed for a quick shower and sauna before gathering up my kids.

As I walked into the locker room there they were coming to get me synchronistically (the timing was perfect!) since Madison had been "run out of the kids' exercise room" by some thirteen-year-old boys who she claimed had crushes on her and were therefore challenging for her to be around. "Oh, I'm back in the Vortex," I sighed with a smile. The synchronicities were happening again. You'll know you're in the Vortex and on the path to creating the best life ever when the Universe sprinkles synchronicities throughout your everyday experiences.

As I toweled off and talked to my sweet children, the former Prana student from the treadmill showed up and was as kind as could be, giving me tips on the monthly towel service, renting a locker, and other things "Y."

"Yes, I'm over the negative energy I brought to myself," I thought with relief. I also told my children the same thing because I'm always teaching them about The Law of Attraction and Deliberate Creation.

On our way out, I sought out the two women at the front desk who I'd been a total bitch to, and apologized. "I'm sorry I was a bitch to you," I said simply. "And I won't ruin my apology with an excuse." "You weren't a bitch," they both chimed in. "Oh yes, I was," I smiled.

We drove home, walked into the house, began eating our raw vegan treats from Prana Restaurant, and started to unpack a huge box full of hand-me-down teeny tiny baby boy clothes that a friend had dropped by. "I'm back," I smiled, as my body relaxed into the well being that is my birthright, and yours.

The lesson? When you practice Deliberate Creation as well as Practices one and three, and really understand and utilize the Law of Attraction moment to moment, your "stream" moves very fast. And a car driving a hundred miles an hour that hits a tree is in a lot more trouble than a car driving five miles an hour.

But it's so fun to drive a hundred miles an hour (metaphorically)! It makes the "ride" that much more exciting and joyful. So I'll continue to move fast down this stream of life, but I'll be ever more cognizant of my thoughts, choosing that which I want and letting go of that which I don't, utilizing Deliberate Creation. No matter what those around me are doing.

# Chapter 58
# Lineage

Be a powerful example by being aligned.

"So and so comes from a long lineage of yoga instructors...." When I read or hear this, a few things come to mind. "Wow, how nice for that person that they had yoga in their life from day one or even while in utero. Rock on. I'm happy for them that they were blessed to be born into that 'lineage.'"

What also comes to mind is how sometimes this statement can be used as a type of exclusion. A type of "I'm a 'better' yogi than you and there's nothing you can do about it because it's in my genes and my 'lineage' and it's not in yours." Just another form of exclusion, arrogance, and ego wrapped up in a yoga mat and scented with incense.

I can see this kinda stuff a mile away and it reminds me of some of the clinical work I did at Harvard while working toward my doctorate in clinical psychology. Occasionally I would observe clinicians playing this card—the "lineage" card. To me, it said to every psychologist who hadn't been so blessed with "lineage," "Sorry, kid. No matter how much you study, how hard you work, how smart you are, how committed you are, how wonderful you are with clients, how talented you are and how much you love this work, you'll just have to wait till the next lifetime because you don't have 'lineage.'"

So even in helping professions and the yoga world, exclusion and arrogance can rear their ugly heads and keep people from simple truth.

The simple truth is that everyone is a yogi and yoga is simply a form of union. Your yoga might look different than my yoga, but everyone can practice yoga daily and it will help them come back to their center and remember who they are so they can walk through the world with integrity and grace.

> The simple truth is that everyone is a yogi and yoga is simply a form of union.

Your "yoga" might be gardening, reading, going for a walk in nature, or baking apple muffins. My yoga is asana (poses) in a heated room every day. Even though to some it sounds scary, I gotta tell ya that this yoga that I practice daily is for everyone. Not just the flexible. Not just the young. Not just the thin. Not just those donning fancy yoga clothes.

Every day I tell someone—at Trader Joe's or the public library or the park or the parking lot of our fourteen-year-old daughter's middle school—this yoga is for you. Just show up and get on your mat and do your best with breath. That's it! You'll feel so good. Whether you have "lineage" or not.

# Chapter 59
# Yoga Journal

Train your point of attraction.

PHOTO: RAY MUCCI

When I began my dedicated, daily yoga practice, I was so "hooked" that I began reading everything I could about this 5000-year-old practice, including Yoga Journal. It didn't occur to me that Yoga Journal is actually "media," because I figured that it was yoga after all. So I read it for a while, devouring every word of wisdom I could glean from its pages.

But in time I noticed that this magazine, yogic or not, was not creating the best mood and the best day ever for me. I noticed that I began to feel the same feelings of insecurity, doubt, and overall fear that I used to feel after reading mainstream magazines. "How could this be?" I asked myself. "This is Yoga Journal!"

Then it occurred to me that any industry can become laden with the same heaviness and darkness that sometimes accompanies "the corporate world" and "the Matrix" (i.e. the "mainstream world"). I recalled one of my first yoga teachers talking in class many years ago about how the "yoga world" can become just as "dark," just as "corrupt," just as "competitive" as any other "world." At the time of that class I wasn't in a place to take in this wisdom so I was dubious. I tucked it away in my psyche to revisit later. And upon revisiting, I realized that what he'd said was true.

My beloved Yoga Journal had become something I couldn't stomach anymore; laden with ads for things I didn't believe in, not-so-veiled hints at competition, and pretty much anything to bring in the all-mighty dollar.

Not that there's anything wrong with abundance. Abundance rocks! But at what "cost?" At the cost of making people feel "less than?" At the cost of making people feel insecure? At the cost of making people feel "left out" unless they do, buy, or "are" this or that?

# Competition is not real and represents the dark side.

This yogi says, "not so much." Totally unnecessary. We can all live in joy and prosper and support and inspire each other without falling into the trap of needing to make others feel less than optimal. When you feel good, I "win" and when I feel good, you "win." This is how abundance, The Law of Attraction, and Deliberate Creation work. No one loses when you "win," and so there's no need to compete. In fact, competing is the antithesis of creating the best life ever and also the antithesis of yoga. Competition is not real and represents the dark side.

I don't read Yoga Journal anymore. Not that there's anything wrong with it. If you feel good while or after you read it, rock on! Only do what makes you happy—the essence of the three Practices of creating the best life ever.

# Chapter 60
# Cleaning and Cleansing

PHOTO: KELLY LORENZ

## Nothing responds as quickly to your patterns of thought as your physical body.

"Once we were in D.C. and we went on two subways and walked two miles to get my Mom a green juice, because she's not quite herself till she's done her practice and had her green juice." So said Madison, our then ten-year-old, while we were giving a raw food talk at one of our yoga studios.

I do drink green juice every day because I love it. We joke in our house that Mommy after she takes a sip of her green juice is like a chain smoker after they take their first hit off of a much-needed cigarette.

If I clean my juicer right after I juice, it's easy. Everything rinses off quickly, the way that butter melts easily in a hot pan. The longer I wait to clean it, the harder it is to get that green stuff off.

If I upload the photos I take regularly and put them in my Shutterfly albums when I upload them, it takes two minutes. If I wait and they build up, it becomes overwhelming, not fun, and takes what seems like a very long time.

And so it is with our bodies and our minds. Practice yoga daily, think thoughts and speak words that make you feel good (Deliberate Creation), and put foods you love in moderation in your body daily. Breathe in and breathe out. Listen to your body and rest when it needs it. Speak your truth, with love. Do something nice for someone else without asking for or expecting anything in return.

Don't wait till you have a crisis—a physical crisis, a mental crisis, an emotional crisis, or a Spiritual crisis to "clean house." Clean house daily. Your physical, mental, emotional, and Spiritual houses.

# Chapter 61
# The Nausea

Focus on what you want and ignore the rest.

When I got pregnant with my first child Madison (now fourteen), I proclaimed with a smug smile at five weeks pregnant that I wasn't nauseous at all and the whole "nausea thing" must be in all "those other" pregnant women's heads. Spoken like a true rookie pregnant Super-mom at only five weeks pregnant.

The following week it hit me.

Oh. My. God. Never had I felt nausea like this and it wasn't morning sickness at all. It was all day, all night, every day, and every night sickness. "Who named this morning sickness anyhow?" I asked angrily. "Must've been a male doctor!"

I felt horrible about having said that silly thing about all of the other Super-moms who've had nausea, swore to The Universe that I was sorry, and begged to have the feeling leave my body,

"Now, please!"

It didn't.

I searched frantically for some relief. I read everything and tried everything. It didn't budge. At twenty-six weeks pregnant—yes, twenty-six weeks—I began to feel better.

If you've ever had nausea with pregnancy, you know that people soon grow tired of hearing about it. They say things like, "Oh, well, don't worry, it'll be gone in three months."

Three months? Have you ever had the flu for three months?

Yeah, there's no sympathy for the nauseous pregnant Super-mom. It just ain't out there so don't bother lookin.

Baby number two, Sagey (now eight-years-old): same nausea, same reactions from others.

Tried everything and nothing worked. Woke up every morning and declared to Philippe, "Today's the day! I'm going to feel great today!" utilizing Deliberate Creation. Then night after night I would lie on the hard wood floor of our dining room sobbing, "Why, why, why won't this stop?"

Baby number three, Phoenix (now five-years-old): same thing. My clearest memory with Phoenix's pregnancy is practicing yoga on the deck at our Beach Club on Nantucket overlooking the breathtaking ocean. I was in the middle of a Sun Salutation A when it hit me—the unmistakable need to throw up. I glanced in the direction of the bathroom and calculated the time it would take to get there, taking into account the fact that I'd need to run by many tables of brunching club goers, and decided to duck under the deck instead and throw up there. Thank goodness I had that good judgment because there's no way I would've made it to the loo, and oh those brunchers would've lost their appetite for lox 'n' bagels 'n' blueberry pancakes.

Yeah, it wasn't just nausea during my first three pregnancies, it was daily vomiting. Usually about twenty times a day. That's usually where most people say, "Oh that's horrible! You poor thing!" Throwing up gets people's attention and garners pity; but the nausea is ten times worse. For me, when I'm pregnant, the throwing up is fast and I actually feel relief for fifteen minutes after I throw up. The nausea is omnipresent and relentless. No relief.

So why write about this in a book called "Create The Best Life Ever?" What could this possibly have to do with you and creating the life of your dreams? I'm getting to that, but I need to explain a bit more first.

At age forty-four I was pregnant with twin boys. That pretty much put me in the category of "Girl, you gonna be realllllly nauseous and there ain't no way around it. Two babies=double the nausea."

But, sit down for this one. I licked it. And here's how.

When the nausea hit, and oh, did it, instead of fighting it, resisting it, and crying about it, I leaned into it, breathed into it, and allowed it (an important part of Deliberate Creation—surrender). Dealing with pregnancy nausea, it turns out, is not unlike manifesting. When we manifest, we ask for something, and we allow it to happen. That's all that's involved. The Universe then takes care of it—immediately and easily. "Then why doesn't everything I ask for manifest immediately?" you ask.

Because you are resisting it in some way, shape, or form. It might be a thought, your words, or your emotions, and they might be unconscious, but you're resisting.

As was I. I was resisting the nausea, just like I resisted the pain of the intense contractions of labor during my first two children's births. And resisting the contractions—the pain—amplified it and made it unbearable.

But with my third child, Phoenix, I allowed the contractions during labor, focused on them, breathed into them, and was therefore able to give birth to my son completely naturally and silently and in less than three hours with only two pushes whereas my labor with Madison was thirty-six hours with two hours and fifteen minutes of pushing and my labor with Sagey was nine hours and I can't remember how much pushing.

So with my twin pregnancy, when I felt the nausea, I acknowledged it, breathed into it, and took it easy. I rested more and complained and talked about it less, distracting myself with other things (Deliberate Creation).

And when I had moments of feeling OK, I acknowledged them. I realized that I did have moments of feeling OK and I learned to focus on them primarily, ignoring the many other moments of not feeling OK.

The nausea was not only easier than in any of my previous pregnancies, but it ended at eleven weeks. Eleven weeks! I was in a state of euphoric shock that morning when I woke up and it was gone—as long as I continued to eat tiny amounts of easy-to-digest food that I could stomach every ten to twenty minutes.

So it took me four pregnancies to "get it." To "get" that Deliberate Creation works in every single situation in my life, and yours. Even dealing with nausea during pregnancy.

So take a look at what's difficult in your life right now. Visualize the way you want it to be, not how it is now. Think about it, talk about it, feel it—how you want it to be. Feel the essence of how you want it to be, utilizing Deliberate Creation. And lean into that. Breathe. Believe. Stop resisting. Then smile because your miracle is on its way.

# Chapter 62
# The Ultrasound

F.E.A.R. = False Expectations Appearing Real

When you are seven months pregnant with twins you frequently underestimate the size of your belly. Or at least this Super-mom did. One night when I was seven months pregnant, I was reaching over to turn out a light and I smacked my pregnant belly on the corner of a chair. A pretty sharp corner. "Ouch!" I blurted out loud. Philippe asked me if I was OK. "I'm fine," I assured him, but after I'd uttered the words, my mind began to go to "work." The "work" that the mind is commissioned to do: cause suffering.

At this point in my life after many hours of yoga asana, affirmations, meditation, and setting of intentions, I'm pretty fearless. Add to these practices a childhood that makes pretty much anything seem like a piece'o cake, fear ain't something I experience often. But when I knocked my belly, those awful feelings of fear resurfaced. Fast. And the thoughts. You know the ones. Not the best ever.

We were staying at a hotel in Boston at the time on a "staycation." After "the bump" we watched a movie, during which I got my mind off of it for a while, but when I woke up in the morning, I felt a little cramp in the place where I'd knocked my pregnant belly. Attempting to stay calm and nonreactive, I stayed in bed for as long as I could, hoping the pain would diminish.

It didn't. It wasn't bad pain but it was pain nevertheless. "Am I creating this pain with my mind?" I wondered.

Later Philippe, the kids, and I swam in the hotel pool, walked on the treadmills in the gym, and practiced yoga, and I was relieved to notice that the cramp had gone away. Whew!

Then it came back.

I called my midwives and the on-call midwife assured me that I was fine, but offered an ultrasound that afternoon for reassurance. "I'll take it!" I said and we quickly packed up.

As I drove to the hospital to confirm that everything was great with my twin sons in my belly, that awful speediness of fear filled my body. I felt shaky, distracted, and sick. I had no appetite. I knew in my heart that my baby boys were fine, yet my mind was messin' with my intuition.

Philippe and the kids had gone home because they had play dates and commitments and I knew that they didn't need to be at the ultrasound because all would be well. When I arrived at the hospital I was greeted in the ultrasound check in area by two of my "ultrasound check-in Sisters," who joked about how big my belly was growing, asked me if I brought them any food from our restaurant (which we still owned at the time), and asked me (again) if I really practiced yoga everyday, bemoaning how they needed to lose weight but were so unmotivated.

I smiled and gave them each a(nother) free pass to Prana Power Yoga and said they'd be so happy when they practiced. They'd feel so good, find more patience and joy, and lose the weight too.

I felt as though I must've been transparent. I was attempting to act "normal" but felt as phony as phony could be as I faked a smile while my lips quivered in fear. But my ultrasound check-in Sisters didn't pick up on it. (They haven't started yoga yet.)

Off they sent me to "radiology...downstairs. I'll show you where it is," said one of my ultrasound check-in Sisters. Oh, I knew where it was. I'd been there once before, and it had not been a good experience. It was the previous May. The ultrasound from Hell that I didn't care to remember.

Attempting to wipe that memory from my mind, I checked in at radiology and joined about seven other patients waiting in the waiting room. These people were sick—very sick—and I could feel it. This was not the energy of the midwives' ultrasound waiting room upstairs. Why had I created this situation?

I began doing anything I could to take my mind off of the situation—texting, emailing, scheduling on my iPhone—anything I could do to keep from shaking—and thinking.

"Taylor?" an ultrasound technician inquired. "That's me," I smiled, as she ushered me—you guessed it—into the exact same ultrasound room I'd been in the previous May when I'd had my miscarriage. Out of eleven ultrasound rooms she brought me into that one. Ugh.

"Ohhhhh! I get it!" I laughed out loud. "I know why I created this! I'm going to recreate my experience in this ultrasound room and have a great experience this time. I'm going to 'close the circle' with joy," I continued. The tech just smiled at me.

As she scanned my babies, she smiled and chatted the whole time, unlike my last time in this room when the technician didn't breathe a word.

"Your twins look great!" she exclaimed immediately. "Wow, they move around a lot! Your placenta looks perfect."

The fear left my body. The word joy doesn't even begin to capture my emotion in that moment. She asked me "what I did" because, "You look thirty, not forty-four!" and I started talking about the three Practices. I felt like I was "home," even in that ultrasound room in the radiology department of a hospital.

"Thank you, thank you, thank you, thank you" I squealed repeatedly with joy and gratitude as I drove home just minutes later. Then the wisdom came—the "other" reason I'd created this experience.

It was gone! The fear of labor I'd been carrying around with me for seven months was completely gone. After the fear I'd just experienced, what's a few hours of (excruciating) labor pain?

Amazing, isn't it, what we bring into our experience to let go of fear to create the best life ever?

# Chapter 63
# Sharing

"Example is not the main thing in
influencing others. It is the only thing."
- Albert Schweitzer

My family and I were at the beach one sunny July day and the sand was packed with happy beach-goers soaking up the sun, splashing in the water, and playing with sand toys. Phoenix, our (then) one-year-old, set his sights on a dump truck that a little boy was playing with and innocently went over to join in on the fun. Matthew, the three-year-old proud owner of the dump truck, snatched it out of Phoenix's little hands and said, "That's my dump truck. Leave it alone!"

The Super-mom of Matthew saw the interaction, was mortified, ran over, and explained to her son, "Honey, you need to share with this little boy. He's just a little guy. He doesn't know it's your dump truck. Be nice and share with the baby."

She handed the dump truck to Phoenix, who happily accepted the navy blue treasure, and began making dump truck noises as he pushed it across the sand. Matthew's Super-mom turned her back for a second and round two began: Matthew snatched the dump truck out of Phoenix's hands—more aggressively this time—reiterating his previous warning with anger, "My dump truck! Leave it alone!"

Hearing the interaction, his Super-mom turned around and intervened again, "Matthew, you must share. That's the right thing to do. Give the baby the dump truck. You can both play with it," she continued as she pried the plastic gold out of her three-year-old's hands and gave it to Phoenix, who smiled with delight.

More dump truck sounds, a very angry look from Matthew and the drama continued as the stakes became higher: the 3-year-old grabbed the dump truck from Phoenix's hands and shoved Phoenix to the ground in full view of his Super-mom. She pulled the truck out of her son's hands, handed it to Phoenix, and repeated her previous words about the importance of sharing. Matthew was not amused or interested in this lesson and continued to assert his boundary with his truck.

Eventually, after a few more go-arounds, Matthew's Super-mom removed her son from the scene. She and Matthew walked up the beach, returning later to apologize to Phoenix and me about Matthew's behavior.

I smiled and told her not to worry. That she was a Super-mom and she did a great job doing her job—teaching her son with love. I told her that she had planted the seeds, whether it felt like her son had heard the lesson or not.

She smiled with relief and seemed amused by the "Super-mom" concept. I explained that we're all Super-moms, whether we know it or not. And sometimes we don't know for a very long time whether the seeds of our teaching "took" or not, but they're there and that's all we can do. Except let go. The letting go can be the most challenging part. Letting go of our expectations, our attachments, our pride, our ego (Yoga is helpful in this process). Letting go of our embarrassment

PHOTO: KELLY LORENZ

when our child behaves in a way that we don't agree with—that wasn't part of the "parenting plan."

How will we respond when our child behaves this way? He is watching us—always—how will we respond? Not just our words but also our energy. How will it play out in a situation where things don't go "as planned?" This is when our children are really watching and really learning, by our words, our actions, and our energy. This is where we are planting the deepest seeds.

What do we teach our children when we are attached to material things, to our ideas, to our fear? What do we teach our children when we believe in scarcity instead of abundance? When we hoard our resources, our money, our time, our food, and our love?

Be mindful Super-mom, your child is watching.

# Chapter 64
# The Treadmill

Reclaim your power. Your Prana. Your life force.

Do you walk on a treadmill? Do the Stairmaster? The elliptical? Row on a rowing machine? Back in the day I used to love walking on a treadmill. I'd walk on the treadmill at my gym and read flashcards while studying for the GREs. I remember once a guy walking on the treadmill next to me offered me a job at his company because he was "so impressed" with my multitasking ability. At first I was proud, but after talking to him for a few minutes, I realized this was just another pickup line. Disgusted, I joined an all-women's gym.

When I was in my doctoral program for clinical psychology, I was super-abundant with my full-time classes and my practicum, so I took the leap and bought my very own treadmill to save time. This way I didn't have to schlep to a gym, park, sign up for a machine, and deal with various other things like pick-up lines and energy. I could just hop on whenever I wanted. I loved it and walked to alleviate the stress of graduate school. When I was pregnant with my first child, I walked to distract myself from the intense nausea. When Madison (now fourteen) was born I walked with her on my chest in a Baby Bjorn to rock her to sleep. Man, I loved that treadmill. I used it every day.

Fast forward to my first yoga practice. I was blown away. It was like nothing I'd ever experienced in this lifetime, and I knew instantly it was my dharma. I knew it from that first practice. From that moment on, due to time constraints of my doctoral program and Super-momhood, I had a choice to make daily: practicing yoga or walking on my treadmill. I didn't have time for both. My yoga practice won hands down.

Since that time I've had an epiphany about treadmills and other such cardio. While walking through the cardio room at the Y the other day to get to the pool to swim it hit me: these machines go nowhere. There's no fresh air in this room. Some of these people are pretty disconnected and almost "trance-like" as they stare at the TVs hooked up to all of these cardio machines. Some of their Spirits are on the back burner. And the irony is, when they finish their workouts, they sometimes walk, sweat drenched, to the elevator to take it one flight down to the locker room.

I'm not sayin' that exercising is bad, or more specifically, that exercising on a cardio machine is bad. I actually love it. I love cardio and I wrote some of this book and have written many a blog and Prana Power Yoga email while on cardio. I'm pointing out the irony and the metaphor. The irony is that as a culture, we pay money to drive to a place and park and change and sign up for a machine and "work out," only to then take an elevator one floor up or down, circle the parking lot for the "perfect spot" at the supermarket so we don't have to walk another fifty steps, and shake our head no to our child's plea to run, jump, and slide with them at the park, preferring to sit on the park bench instead.

Our bodies need to move. Our Spirits need to move energy. Our bodies and minds need fresh air. And for those of us who live where there are long, cold winter months, doing this can be a challenge. I hear that. So it's not about "don't get on cardio." It's about being mindful, being aware, and seeing what you are looking at (yoga really helps with this). Move your body in all the ways you can, not just that X number of minutes on a machine.

The metaphor? Our Spirits need to be heard. Our Spirits need us to move energy. Our Spirits need us to be grounded and centered. But we often don't take the time to sit down, close our eyes, and get centered. We argue that we "don't have time" for a yoga practice. We "don't have time" to prepare and enjoy the foods we love in moderation and without restriction. If I had a nickel for every time I heard, "I skip breakfast and lunch because I don't have time...."

Reclaim your power. Your Prana. It's right there inside you waiting to be found once you utilize the three Practices regularly.

# Chapter 65
# The Shame Core

"Love is what we were born with.
Fear is what we learned here."
- Marianne Williamson

The shame core. Yes, you have one. We all do. Never heard of it? Don't know what I'm talking about? I'll explain and help you relieve some of the pain it causes.

How do you feel when a friend, colleague, or acquaintance has something really great happen to them? Do you feel joy for them? Excited for them? Proud of them? Inspired by them?

Or perhaps a little jealousy creeps in...or anger...or confusion...or competition? If you said yes to anything that doesn't feel good, your shame core is at work.

When we are born, we are perfect, joyful little beings. And we know it! We know we got it goin' on, even though we are pudgy little people with bald heads, no teeth, and perhaps a poop in our pants if we haven't been changed lately. We know we are beautiful, powerful, and perfect, and we're not afraid to ask for what we want. If we're mad, we immediately let people know. We scream until we get what we want (love, food, sleep, a diaper change). And you know what? People listen. They don't judge us for asking for what we want. They don't get angry with us. They aren't jealous of us for getting what we want. They don't feel confused or competitive. In fact, people adore us. They love being around us because we are pure light. We have not yet been conditioned to have shame or guilt about anything.

Fast-forward a few decades.

My, how things have changed. The reasons that the shame core began and grew or didn't grow are different for us all. But every single human being walking this

planet, no matter how "accomplished," has a shame core. The question is, how often do you listen to it and let it rule or more accurately ruin your life?

I saw a movie called "Shrink," with Kevin Spacey. It was a bit dark but well done and a good look at this issue that pervades many an interaction happening on the planet. Spacey is a therapist to the stars and quite "successful." He has a bestselling book, named, quite ironically, "Happiness." Why is this ironic? Because Spacey is miserable. His wife committed suicide (unbeknownst to many —even his father and friends—because he told everyone that she was in a car accident) and he is hanging on by a thread, smoking weed several times a day to self-medicate.

At one point in the film, Spacey says on national television that he is a fraud, that happiness doesn't exist, and that his wife killed herself. He says that no one should buy his book as he rips a copy of it to shreds on camera.

"Now his book will really sell," I said to Philippe.

What happened then? Did his book sell as I predicted?

What happened was that once Spacey "came clean," spoke his truth, and hit rock bottom once he shined the light on his deep, dark, shame core and could literally go no lower. Then he began to heal and come out of the darkness.

It's all about awareness. But how can we be aware? For me, yoga has been one of the most transformative practices in my life, in addition to Practices two and three of creating the best life ever. Your yoga practice can and will uncover stuck energy that's holding you back from your pure potential. It will make you aware and shine the light on your shame core.

Different people have different types of "yoga." For me and thousands of others it's Prana Power Yoga. Maybe for you it's gardening, walking in nature, taking a hot bath with candles, meditating, reading, or writing. You know, or you will know. Experiment and see. What brings you back to your center and helps you remember who you are, without that shame core? What is the "yoga" for you that helps you to find the awareness that will set you free?

Once the feelings come up, the "I'm not good enough," "Why does he do so well?" "When is it my turn?", "I should've done more school," "I'm not smart enough," "No

one likes me," "I'm not popular enough," "My body's not right," etc. . . stop. Get quiet and identify what's going on. What's really going on. It's not about the other person. It's about you, and your shame core.

But no worries. That's not who you are. Rewind back to the adorable little baby who was so in her power that nothing stopped her from getting what she wanted and needed. That's who you are. Pure joy. Pure light. Pure love. Pure potential. Pure Prana.

Love is what you were born with. Fear is what you learned here. Anything can be unlearned.

How? Find "your" yoga. Change your thoughts. Put only foods you love in moderation into your body. Whenever possible only hang out with people who make you feel good.

"That's impossible!" you say. "I hate my boss, my mother-in law, my co-workers...."

Now those are exactly the type of thoughts to which I was referring.

Start small. Change each thought to one that feels a little bit better (Deliberate Creation). For example, "Well, my mind is saying that's impossible, but I can try this and see what happens. I have nothing to lose, except the fear and suffering."

There you go. You're on the path and you're doin great!

# Chapter 66
# The Rorschach

"Don't take anything personally. Nothing others do is because of you. What others say and do is a projection of their own reality, their own dream. When you are immune to the opinions and actions of others, you won't be the victim of needless suffering"
- Miguel Ruiz

PHOTO: RAY MUCCI

When I was pregnant with Sagey (now eight-years-old), I had a very interesting and illuminating experience. I taught and practiced Prana Power Yoga every day until the day I delivered her, and while teaching received many a comment on my blossoming belly. "You're huge!" a student exclaimed at the beginning of a class. Then at the end of the very same class a different student told me how "tiny" I was.

At first this threw me off a bit. I wasn't used to anyone calling me "huge" (who is?), and people's disregard for tact and my feelings were un-nerving to me, especially with all of those hormones surging through my body.

Once a student said loudly to me in front of fifty other students, "You're so huge already! My daughter is due at the same time you are and she's not even showing yet!"

How, I ask, is a Super-mom supposed to respond to that with grace? I did my best, with breath. I smiled, took a deep breath in and out, and began teaching class.

It's amazing how people feel that they can rightfully comment on the size of a pregnant woman when they would never say the same words to someone not carrying a baby (or multiples). No one would approach an overweight person and exclaim, "You're huge!"

Yet many a person felt inclined to tell me their gauge of where I was physically, every step along my pregnancy paths. All five of them. And the most bizarre part of it was that their descriptions varied so widely, even on the very same day.

One night, when telling Philippe about this phenomenon, it occurred to us what was going on. I had become a human Rorschach test. When people looked at me, their sense of their own body came pouring out, rather uncontrollably it seemed. So with this new understanding, the speaker's own body image became obvious to me by how they described my pregnant body.

"You're tiny!" or "You look great!" meant that they felt confident and happy with their body. "You're huge!" meant they felt the same way about themselves. In short, I had become a big (pun intended) screen for my student's projections. And, apparently, the fact that I was pregnant made it feel "appropriate" for them to blurt out these projections.

With my next pregnancy (with Phoenix, now age five), I was prepared. It didn't faze me when people commented. It was simply my window into their psyche.

When pregnant with my twin boys I actually had fun with it—this view into others' minds. For example, one day a very thin member of our Prana Restaurant staff (which we still owned at the time) remarked repeatedly how huge my belly was, how she couldn't believe it was going to keep getting bigger, and how she thought I looked like I was going to pop. I smiled as I listened, and sent her light, poor love, because if my Rorschach theory was correct, I knew that even though her physical body was small, she didn't feel that way inside.

What we believe about ourselves we see in others. So the next time someone comments on your physicality, smile, take a breath, and remember that it really has nothing to do with you.

# Chapter 67
# Freedom

"The secret of happiness is freedom.
The secret of freedom is courage."
- Thucydides

Joy and freedom are interlinked. In order to have joy we must have freedom, and when we have freedom, we are joyful.

Yoga teaches us that we are free—that in any situation we always have a choice. Even if we feel stuck, imprisoned, etc., we can choose otherwise.

I loved my ex-husband dearly and will always love him. He was my first true love, we were together for eighteen years, and we created a beautiful child together whom we co-parent.

But we were and are as different as different can be. I always thought love was enough but learned differently as I began to feel my freedom slipping away. It was insidious so I couldn't place my finger on the malaise that was consuming me.

Then I found yoga, remembered who I was and why I'm on this planet, and found freedom and joy again. I did have a choice in every moment about which thought I would focus on.

Little children are totally free. Watch them! They are free with their love, their anger, and their fear. Their entire being exudes freedom. They are free to be themselves, be honest, ask if they don't know something, cry if they feel like it, and lie down on the hardwood floor in the kitchen and go to sleep amongst a big party if the mood so strikes them. They are confident about who they are and they love who they are. They are living the best life ever and they would never think that it should be otherwise.

When does this shift? When do we begin to fear being wrong, not knowing the answer, showing our emotions, showing our true self? When does the freedom that is our birthright begin to slip away?

Every year we train fifty teachers in our Prana Power Yoga Teacher Training. During our 200 hours together, we talk a lot about joy and freedom. Students often talk about a moment in their childhood when they recall that self-confidence, that freedom, that joy slipping away. We teach about the beauty of beginning again—that with awareness (as you now have after reading this) we can make the choice to begin again and regain our freedom and our joy.

It's your birthright, so start now.

# Chapter 68
# The Snow Storm

What you focus on becomes dominant in your life.

PHOTO: PHILIPPE WELLS

One night I giggled as I heard Philippe and Madison (age thirteen at the time) argue about the ability of her middle school to predict the weather. There was a winter storm watch and her school had called an early release day. School was going to be let out before lunch. Madison was busy making sledding and hot chocolate plans with her friends as Philippe and I explained to her that it was weather so no one knew what would actually go down, and that we had an inkling we would get no snow at all. This is not what she wanted to hear as she texted five friends, inviting them to our house to sled, drink hot chocolate, and sit by the fire.

Her reasoning for her unshakable "snowstorm confidence?" "My school knows what they're doing. They have never been wrong. If they made it a half day, it's going to snow."

"Then," Philippe quipped, "Your school needs to be consulting with the National Weather Service because they have a much better record than the Weather Service and they need to make money off of this not very well known strength of theirs."

Madison looked at me, and we both smiled at her Papa's amazing sense of humor and wit.

Philippe and I didn't cancel classes at our Prana Power Yoga Studios because of the impending storm. We've learned. We wait, we watch, and we meditate on it.

No snow came. It rained a bit and was very windy, but no snow. I was at an appointment at my chiropractor's and running an errand for Sagey's upcoming birthday party and got a call from Philippe explaining that one of our Prana teachers "didn't feel comfortable" teaching her class that evening at one of our yoga studios. "It's raining!" I laughed as I drove down the street effortlessly. "There's absolutely no snow!" "I know," Philippe said, "but she's saying she can't teach."

We'd had "issues" with this teacher before. But I really liked her and always stuck up for her when "stuff" came up—when she didn't do her fair share at the studios, when she had an attitude with other Prana teachers, when she didn't show up to teach a class and then argued about the "no show protocol".

Philippe stepped up and taught her class on that rainy night. It was the eleventh hour and we weren't going to get into it with this teacher and then have her show up to deliver a class without inspiration and with attitude.

That night as we went to sleep, we asked the Universe for clarity on what action to take regarding this teacher. When the clarity came, we followed it and then let the whole thing go, without getting angry or frustrated. This is the practice of Deliberate Creation—focusing on what we want and ignoring the rest, while remaining in line with our responsibilities.

It's our job to teach by our example. By walking our talk. By living our dharma—our yoga. By creating deliberately. "My life is my message" is one of my favorite quotes.

To get all worked up about this situation would've created drama and bad energy, and invited The Law of Attraction to draw more of that to us. And we have a choice.

Instead we focused on the good (we have so many amazing teachers teaching at Prana who don't do this type of thing), asked for guidance, and left the rest up to the Universe. It does a better job than we ever do.

There is always going to be "contrast" in your life. How will you respond?

# Chapter 69
# A Little Help From My Friends

"What do I do when my love is away
(Does it worry you to be alone)?
How do I feel by the end of the day
(Are you sad because you're on your own)?
No, I get by with a little help from my friends."
- The Beatles

When I was in my third trimester of my pregnancy with twin boys I joyfully and gratefully welcomed the extra sleep and food I needed as my little guys grew like weeds in my burgeoning belly. I was so grateful to have made it to that point of my best pregnancy ever while feeling great, positive, hopeful, and excited for the two divine beings who would walk the earth with our family and me in just a few short months. Along with the joy and gratitude of moving into trimester three healthfully, came a need to slow down even more and consequently ask for help even more often.

After Phoenix's third birthday celebration with good friends—raw coconut cream pie and ice cream, balloons, and a few small presents (this kid is overjoyed with receiving one "Match box" car and so I've learned, as with everything, less is more)—Philippe jumped on the train to visit our Prana NYC Yoga Studio and teach a few classes.

In previous months, our three kids and I were along for the journey, enjoying hanging out at Prana NYC, teaching, and taking in the Big Apple and all the great raw vegan food (we were all still raw vegan at the time), high energy, and culture it provides. But since I'd been pregnant with the twins and dialed everything down significantly, I'd taken a sabbatical from teaching, mostly because of the energy it takes to talk for sixty to ninety straight minutes and the lack of oxygen that I had after attempting to do so (because of the increase in blood flow when you're pregnant). So Philippe journeyed solo that weekend and I stayed home with our three kiddos.

I'd been gratefully used to having my soul mate "around" all the time (unless one of us was teaching) because we run our five Prana Power Yoga Studios out of our home and were home schooling Sagey and Phoenix at the time. At first it was weird not to have him there with us that weekend. But adversity throughout my childhood taught me well how to adjust instantly to any situation, a quality that has served me well. So the kids and I instantly settled into the new dynamic and energy in our home and enjoyed each other's energy with the Wells family of four instead of five.

It's a beautiful thing to miss your soul mate while concurrently enjoying a different dynamic and energy. To be in your power to be with my three kids solo and two babies in your burgeoning belly and also be strong enough to ask for help from your friends. And help I got. When you need it—and ask—help is always there for you. My friends came through.

At that point in my twin pregnancy, practicing Prana Power Yoga while reading my affirmation note cards and listening to Abraham-Hicks was about all my tired pregnant body could physically do in a day. I'd do so in the morning while surrounded by my two little ones doing their home

schooling work, and when I finished my practice and came rolling up to standing, I'd feel a huge sense of accomplishment and relief—"I did it!" I say to myself—with the same joy and pride I feel when we finish training a group of fifty new Prana Power Yoga teachers, teach a group of fifty Prana Cleanse™ students, consult with a client who is open to my teachings and is on her way to the best life ever, teach yoga to a huge group of students to raise money for a cause I believe in, or finish teaching a group of fifty-five Prana students who started out resistant and closed and finished their practice open and rooted in their power and joy.

That's the key to Deliberate Creation—to feel the essence of the joy—no matter what the "cause." And in this case it was finishing my yoga practice, because with a belly that size with two baby boys wriggling inside, it was something I was proud of.

One morning that weekend as I finished my practice I meditated on gratitude—for my three children; my twin boys in my belly; my husband that I was grateful to miss; my practice; all the high-vibration raw food that I was putting into my body every day; our warm, cozy home filled with good energy; and for the support from my friends—especially now while Philippe was away. My friend who brought the kids and me take-out from our restaurant the night before. The friend who agreed to bring her daughter to our home for a play date since Super-mom didn't want to get in the car and schlep anywhere. The friend who drove our then twelve-year-old home from a sleepover at his home for the same reason. The friend who came over to visit with her son later that afternoon, bringing me a pole for the Karma flag she'd given me since I couldn't bear the thought of schlepping to a hardware store. The other friends who offered to bring me what I needed and come to visit while Philippe was in NYC.

Tune into that energy! Tune into that Prana. This is the essence of Deliberate Creation, and talk about power and abundance. Talk about the best life ever.

It's there, all around you, whenever you are open and surrendered enough to ask.

# Chapter 70
# The Reaction

*Watch your thoughts, for they become your words. Watch your words because they become your actions. Watch your actions for they form who you are.*

We have a teenage daughter who's a love. She is wonderful in every way and we are blessed to have her in our lives. This said, lately she's been a bit—ehh—spacey about this and that, and I'll just leave it at that so I don't embarrass her, which apparently I am getting very adept at doing.

Philippe and I believe in focusing on what we do want not what we don't want since whatever we focus on grows; however, because of a few situations of late we found it important for the sake of teaching to set a limit with Madison for a week or so.

She wasn't "grounded," but wasn't allowed to "change the plan" at the very last minute—i.e., the pickup from school plan, the hang out with friends plan, the after school plan, her activity plan, etc. After we talked with her and explained our feelings with love she agreed in her own sweet way.

Fast forward to four days later.

I got a call from Madison on my iPhone. I wasn't home and it was "that pickup from school time of day" and just seeing her number on my phone got me goin.' I was mad.

I answered the phone and before I even let that poor kid speak, launched into, "Madison, you can't change 'the plan.' That was our agreement. It's only day four of seven...."

"Mom, I just wanted to know if I could borrow your ice skates," she replied calmly.

I felt silly and reactive and apologized. She let it go immediately and went back to the subject at hand—could she borrow my skates?

Why do we react instead of respond? Why do we function two steps ahead when where we need to be is in the now, where all the magic and miracles happen? Why didn't I just listen to my daughter instead of interrupting her and speaking "my piece?"

The answer is that we do things that aren't the best ever when we are out of alignment. We react instead of respond when we are not grounded. Every time. When we are in this place of mis-alignment we aren't functioning from our Higher Self or authentic self but from our mental body, which is always going to cause suffering.

How do we insure that we are operating from our center? That we are aligned? That we are grounded? It's a daily practice—a path—and it's important to be gentle with yourself and know that it's what we do most of the time that matters. We all do the very best we can in each moment, according to where we are.

Next, it's important to find something that centers and aligns you and that you enjoy. For many people this is yoga. It's something I've now said repeatedly but it bears repeating again, your "yoga" might be something else: gardening, meditating, running, reading, swimming, cooking, biking, taking a bath, and walking in nature are just a few examples.

Find what grounds you, and do it daily. It takes discipline to do something daily. Cultivate that discipline. We all make time to do what we really want to do.

Next, eat what you love in moderation with no restriction. I don't care how much yoga you've done and are doing, if you are either restricting yourself in the food department or overeating anything—no matter how "healthy" a food it is—on a regular basis, it ain't helping you create the best life ever. Period.

Finally watch your thoughts, for they become your words. Watch your words because they become your actions. Watch your actions for they form who you are. We get what we focus on—wanted or unwanted. It's all about the power of the focus of your mind.

Practice, practice, practice what you're learning in this book, smile, and watch your life transform into the best life ever.

# Chapter 71
# The Big Salad

*I know that I don't have to figure everything out.*
*I know that the path will light up for me.*
*I know that it'll come.*

I was making a big salad a few years ago when I was still donning the "raw vegan" label. I had a lot of abundance in the fridge that day in the greens department, and I wanted to use up as much as possible because my sunflower sprouts and romaine were starting to turn. I put in two packages of sunflower sprouts, some chopped veggies, tomatoes, romaine, avocado, olives, and the best homemade raw salad dressing ever—and tossed.

As I looked at that oh-so-abundant salad in front of me, I smiled as I recalled a time years prior, when we first went 100% raw vegan and I used to say a mantra every time I nursed baby Sagey (an infant at the time) that went something like this, "We have an abundance of delicious, raw vegan food available to us at all times. Everything that we could ever want and need and it's all the best and most delicious ever. We eat anything and everything that we want and as much as we want whenever we want—all raw vegan food—and it all comes to us easily and joyfully."

Now this wasn't actually the case at the time. Not at all. It wasn't an accurate reflection of the "truth" or my "now experience" in that moment. At the time in fact we had no clue about raw vegan food, how to prepare it, where to buy it online, etc., and I had some fear and scarcity issues on the raw food front. I wondered if I'd get "enough" to eat, especially so that I could make the best breast milk ever for my baby, and wondered if I would ever again eat anything except big salads and almond butter.

But now in the present moment that mantra had become a reality. We had "an abundance of delicious raw vegan food available to us at all times and it was the best and most delicious ever and we ate anything and everything that we wanted and as much as we wanted whenever we wanted—all raw vegan food—and it all came to us easily and joyfully."

We knew how to quickly and easily prepare the best raw dishes ever and where to easily (and most economically) get the products to do so. We had learned the best websites to get what we needed to lead an abundant and happy raw vegan lifestyle, and, in fact, created our very own website to offer "the best of the best" products, including our own products from our Prana Restaurant, to make it easier for us and our students, consulting clients, and friends to live a healthier lifestyle joyfully and abundantly.

Back in the day before we owned the restaurant I used to make everything myself because there weren't any raw vegan restaurants in our area and I found preparing raw vegan food enjoyable, relaxing, and easy.

Philippe and I loved the raw-vegan food we made ourselves so much and knew that others would enjoy it as well and figured, "How hard can it be to sell it at our studios?" It turned out not to be hard at all; in fact, whatever we filled our Prana Power Yoga Newton studio fridge with sold out in one day. What was challenging was keeping up with the demand and in time it became clear that we should open a restaurant. This coupled with the fact that we had nowhere to go out to eat in our area to eat raw vegan fare was the inspiration for opening our Prana Restaurant on September 4, 2009.

So while I was eating that big salad, I realized that not a day went by that Philippe and I didn't express gratitude to each other and the Universe for the abundance in our lives—the love, light, joy, and yes, the food that had become so easy for us to fill our home with, even though at one time it was just a mantra I said to myself every time I ate.

So if you want something in some area of your life and there is no evidence of it at this moment, no worries. Focus on what it is that you want, feel the essence of it, and create a mantra that in the present tense describes this essence. Say the mantra often. Fake it till you make it.

Then one day you'll look back and smile, realizing that now that mantra is a reality. And you manifested it. Joyfully and easily, utilizing Deliberate Creation.

# Chapter 72
# The Sleep Schedule

Seize joy moment to moment.

At this point, we all know that time is an illusion. So why then, is it so distressing when we get "off schedule?" Why is it so debilitating when we can't sleep at night? And why, as the minutes and hours tick by, do we grow increasingly agitated as thoughts like, "How am I going to function tomorrow when I need to handle X, Y, and Z?" move through our minds at record speed?

I learned a new skill when I was in my third trimester of my pregnancy with my twin boys. My sleep schedule at that point was, uh, erratic at best. Some nights I'd fall asleep quickly and easily. Other nights I was wide awake, albeit tired, for no apparent reason.

I had a choice in this situation (as I do in every situation in my life): surrender or suffer.

Suffering isn't the best option. I'd then feel stressed, annoyed, frustrated, and powerless.

The surrender option? Much more appealing. I'd just take a minute at a time, stay in the now, and let go of the future. This is the essence of Deliberate Creation.

One night I was tired, couldn't sleep, and didn't feel like writing, working, cleaning, organizing, or anything 'cept sleeping, which I just couldn't do.

Suffering would've included fretting about, "Why can't I sleep?" "How will I function tomorrow?" "I wish I felt like being productive," and so on.

Surrendering meant breathing in and breathing out, noticing the color of the night sky through our bedroom windows, looking at a photo album I made two years ago, meditating, and visualizing the next day without time as an element. All excellent examples of how to utilize Deliberate Creation.

In time, I did fall asleep, but not for long. When you're seven months pregnant with twins you wake up a lot to go potty, and so a few hours later I was up again facing the same challenge.

Choosing to surrender, I noticed that the night sky through our bedroom windows now included a crescent moon, which hadn't been there before. It was a sign of time passing but no fear or stress was associated with it. My mind wandered to things I felt grateful for. My breath deepened. In time (not sure how long, it's super important not to look at a clock), I was asleep again.

Then I was awake again and this time it was light—no night sky and no moon—and so my eyes immediately wandered to the clock, which read 5 am. My mind reasoned that I hadn't slept long enough. My Spirit disagreed.

I surrendered to my Spirit, as always, purposefully ignoring the thoughts of, "You'll be so tired later and won't be able to function." Remember, it's all about the power of the focus of your mind.

On my mat in the darkness of our Buddha room, I had the best practice ever on very few hours of Z's. As I finished my practice it occurred to me that I could sneak over to the Y and swim a half-mile before my three kiddos opened their eyes to the new day. I followed my heart and excitement and before I knew it was in the pool swimming up and back, up and back, breathing, and counting.

Logic would tell you that a woman pregnant with twins at age forty-four wouldn't be able to "function" let alone practice yoga, swim a half mile, and walk on a treadmill on the amount of sleep I'd accrued. But don't tell that to my Spirit.

I was back home before 7:30 am and the house was still quiet. Now I was tired. I smiled as I crawled under my covers, snuggled up, and closed my eyes.

I had no idea how I'd get away with sleeping at that moment since my kids would wake soon, but I seized the (silent) moment and began to catch those Zs that my twin boys were now pulling for.

How does this story end? How long did I get to sleep? How did the rest of my day go? It doesn't really matter, does it? Just like the end of the movie "Swing Vote", although you really want to know whom he voted for, the point of the movie had nothing to do with that. The point of that story—and mine—is the process and seizing joy moment to moment throughout that process. One of the keys to creating the best life ever.

# Chapter 73
## Align Yourself

As I sat down to edit this book, my eyes were distracted from the computer screen by a rainbow of markers lying all over my desk, many with tops off, and paper and toys scattered about. Our one-year-old (at the time) twin sons loved to "help Mommy" in her office, and they had been very busy that morning.

As they napped in their room next to my office, I wasn't focused on editing because of the clutter and so the editing wasn't going well or happening at all.

I got up and cleaned up, breathing in and breathing out as I did so. It took all of one minute.

Then I was aligned and centered and could focus. Time vanished as the words flowed effortlessly onto my Mac screen. This is the timelessness of being in the moment and being focused—in the flow of life.

> This is the timelessness of being in the moment and being focused.

How many times are we distracted, not present, and feeling off-center? For most people, the answer is "a lot." How do we bring ourselves back to the moment, our focus, and our center?

A daily yoga practice helps a lot. Because our practice doesn't end with the last asana (pose). That's actually where it begins. Your yoga is how you move through your day and your world. Will you do so with integrity and grace? Will you be focused on what you are working on, to whom you are listening, your breath in and out?

Or will you be overwhelmed, thinking about the laundry list of things to do in your home and office, emails to be written, bills to be paid, phone calls to return, work to be done?

I'd choose the former. And when you do, you're on your way to creating the best life ever.

# Chapter 74
# Total Alignment

Step into alignment, where your power is.

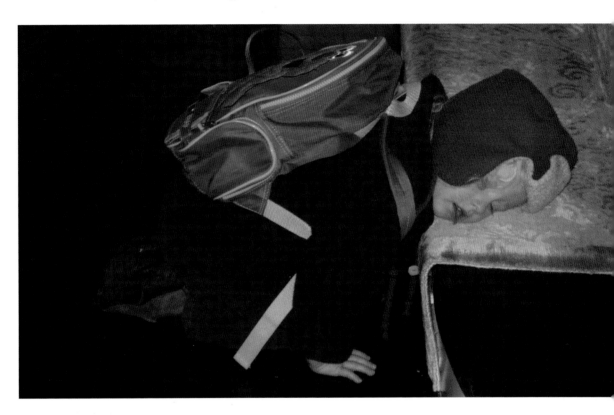

In my fifth month of my twin pregnancy a friend of mine wrote me a message on facebook warning me that she'd dreamt that I'd had my twin boys early. She said she just wanted me to be prepared. "How early?" I asked. "Twenty-nine weeks," she replied.

I took out a calendar, did the math and noticed that the day on which she said I would have my twin sons was our then five-year-old daughter's birthday, February 20th.

"That Universe!" I said out loud as I smiled at the irony and the synchronicity.

I then went into immediate planning mode. "I will go on self prescribed bed-rest the week before she says I'm going to have my twins—week twenty-eight. It'll be better to spend many weeks in bed at home than many weeks in a hospital," I reasoned rationally, operating 100% from my mind since some fear had been generated by her (well-meaning) email. When fear comes up, we often times operate from our mental body. Or at least I do.

In the days that followed I told this story often (when people asked—which was a lot).

I also told Philippe, Madison, Sagey, and Phoenix that they wouldn't be going to Disney World this February vacation as we had planned. I didn't fancy the idea of going into labor all by myself. We usually go to Disney every February vacation with Philippe's family or my brother and his family but this year that wasn't gonna happen, I explained firmly.

Then I started to feel really good in my pregnancy. It was against all logic and odds since I was forty-four and pregnant with twin boys in my third trimester, but I felt fantastic. You're "supposed" to feel best second trimester, but I was going strong in my third. Never mind that my belly looked like it looked the day that I delivered my first three kids. It didn't stop me from swimming a half-mile, practicing a full Prana Power Yoga flow, and walking on the treadmill daily. I felt happy, alive, strong, and confident so I had a change of mind and of plans. Now operating from my Spirit and creating deliberately, I declared on one Tuesday night to Philippe and the kids that they should go to Disney, and leave that Thursday (a day later). "I'll be fine," I assured them. "In fact, I'll be great! I'll swim and practice and walk daily. And I'll finish my book."

They were thrilled, but tentative. "Are you sure?" they asked with love. "I'm sure," I assured them. "I'm having these babies in April or May, not February. Call the airlines."

Philippe did his magic and by the end of the night they had flights at a great price and were booked at the same hotel as their aunt, uncle, and cousins. Everyone was over the moon.

Everything flowed beautifully and easily as it does when you follow your heart and listen to your intuition (instead of others), and as they were packing up in preparation to fly off to Disney World, Philippe called me into the foyer.

There was Phoenix (age three at the time), in his hat, coat, and shoes and with his Elmo backpack strapped to his back, sound asleep on his knees with his head on the first step of the stairs.

"Now that's what it's all about," I said as I took a photo of that precious little guy who'd been going a mile a minute just a few moments before—so excited to see Mickey Mouse—and was now fast asleep, with his bent knees on the hard wood floor and his head on a stair.

"That's total alignment," I explained to Madison (then age twelve) and Sagey (then age five) who walked in to see Philippe and me gazing lovingly at their brother.

Phoenix was totally centered and grounded and so he didn't need the right bed, the right lighting, the right pillow, the right temperature, the right clothes, ear plugs, and the right mood to fall asleep (like someone else I know). Anywhere, anytime, he could be "out" like that. This is the essence of the three Practices working together in unison. This is the best life ever.

Phoenix was effortlessly practicing the art of allowing. There was no resistance in his little body. He hadn't yet learned that it's "his job" to resist.

Phoenix and all children are here to teach us—Philippe, you, and me—to stop resisting and start allowing. Start listening to your intuition and ignoring all the other signals from other (usually well-meaning) people. Your Spirit has a story they know nothing about. Only you know what's best for you, just as only Phoenix knows what's best for him. And he listens. Do you?

# Chapter 75
# The Organizer

Hold your vision.
See it!
And trust the process.

Philippe, Madison, Sagey, and Phoenix were at Disney World and I was home writing—ostensibly finishing this book. I write very quickly and joyfully because it's my dharma, like yoga and teaching. My only challenge at the time was finding the time to write with three kids, four Prana Power Yoga Centers (we hadn't built Prana Brooklyn yet), two blogs, a consulting practice, and a raw vegan restaurant (which we still owned). So this was the perfect opportunity to spend many hours writing with peace and quiet.

This first morning of my four-day sabbatical from caring for my three children my intention was to get on my mat upon waking and then swim, walk, and hit the Mac fully aligned and ready to write. What really happened? I ended up spending the first four hours of my day cleaning, organizing, and filling bags with things to give away. Man, those four hours went by in a heartbeat.

Once in awhile I heard a faint voice in the back of my mind saying, "You should get on your mat and then get to the pool so you can begin writing," but it was faint, and my Spirit is bold and strong. So the joyful and effortless organizing continued.

My kids' homeschooling area needed some love, as did their rooms and our kitchen, and I was having the time of my life. Whatever is giving you joy in any moment is what you "should" be doing in that moment. Living by a "to-do list" ain't where it's at. I can say this because I lived that way—ruled by the never-ending to do list—for over three decades. "From 12-12:15 pm: read English Literature." My roommate from Brown claims that I had written this on a daily schedule for myself that allowed for zero downtime and maximum efficiency. "From 12:15-12:30: talk to Andy" (my boyfriend), it continued (according to her). And girlfriend calls a spade a spade.

To think that I lived that way (in fifteen-minute planned increments) gives me a feeling of sadness and suffocation. That's a prison.

Not that lists or schedules are bad. They have their purpose. But not at the expense of drowning out the voice of your Spirit, which loves freedom and the flow of life.

So now, many years and many yoga practices later, I had my "plan" for the day that day and instead of listening to the details of the plan, which had been created by my mind, I allowed my Spirit to take over and run the show, evidence of the surrender so essential when practicing Deliberate Creation.

I've utilized the three Practices to create the best life ever for long enough now that I know that everything I intend on getting done and more will magically happen but often it's not in the way that my mind thought it would go down. This is the nature of the flow of the Universe. This is the essence of Deliberate Creation and utilizing The Law of Attraction. You set an intention, visualize it, make a plan, and then let go, letting the pieces fall where they may and letting things happen at the time they are meant to happen. Otherwise, you're resisting, and when you put out resistant energy you won't sync with the flow of abundance and the best life ever. It's on a different frequency than resistance.

So think about what you want, see it, feel it, plan it, and then let go. Have faith that the pieces will fall where they need. Have faith that this moment is as it should be. Have faith that the Universe always does a better job creating it than you or I ever do.

Need some faith? Need some help letting go? That's easy. Just get on your mat, and breathe.

# Chapter 76
# The Flow

I let things happen. I don't make things happen.

PHOTO: KELLY LORENZ

While day four of Philippe and my three kids' February 2010 Disney World Adventure drew to a close, dusk surrounded our white castle in Newton, Massachusetts and I was marveling at the flow of the Universe. And how after much practice utilizing the three Practices of creating the best life ever, I'm able to surrender to it.

Years ago, before I utilized the three Practices regularly, I would've had a very different five days away from my family. I would've had every moment planned. And I would've stuck to that schedule no matter what. No matter if I felt like it or not, that schedule would've been the determinant of what went down in this Super-mom's days and nights.

But thanks to a consistent, deliberate, and disciplined utilization of the three Practices, I'm much softer and gentler in general. If I feel like doing something, I do it. If I don't, I don't. I trust in the flow of the Universe and in the guidance of my Higher Self so I know intuitively and confidently that if I don't feel like doing something, the time isn't right to do it even if I had "planned" on doing it at that specific time. I know that if I force myself to do something (i.e., write), it won't flow, will take much longer, and will be much more challenging than if I wait for inspiration to hit.

An example was day four of my four-day sabbatical from caring for my three children. It was the first day of the four days that my family had been away that I had completely "free" to write. The first three days I had had commitments, meetings, consultations, and appointments that took up part of my days and evenings. I was so excited to have a totally open day to channel on my Mac. But when I woke up (after eleven hours of sleep—go Super-mom plus two—sleep on!), I wanted to go swimming.

So I did. I scooted over to the Y and as I walked in, I noticed a sign on the door saying, "Both of the pools will close today at noon for a swim meet. Sorry for the inconvenience."

I glanced at the clock and it was 11:20 am—exactly enough time for me to change into my suit, hop into the pool, and swim a half mile before the meet began.

And so I did, smiling to myself that I had listened to my intuition and my Spirit and gone to the Y for a dip, since had I not, there'd be no dippin' that day because of the meet.

After I finished my laps I hopped on the treadmill to walk a bit and catch up on emails and texts and voicemails on my iPhone while I walked, and I heard a message from a lifestyle nutritionist in NYC who wanted to speak at The Prana Restaurant (which we still owned at the time) in the upcoming week. I called him back and we had a nice chat after he exclaimed, "Your timing is amazing! I was just thinking of you and this is the last time I'll be able to talk today because of commitments!" Rock on, flow of the Universe.

After doing an errand I went home to ostensibly hop on my mat before I began writing. Not so much. Without a thought and any hesitation I began nesting. I framed and hung photos, painted frames for my kids and friends as a surprise, organized, gave stuff away, and cleaned. I was in heaven (I'm a Virgo) and the whole world slipped away, along with several hours of the afternoon.

Yet I felt calm and at peace, knowing that whatever I was doing was the "right thing," as indicated by my emotions, which were positive and calm. Our emotions are our guidance system, so listen to them and you'll always be on the right track and creating the best life ever.

When I grew tired of nesting and felt "done," I hopped on my mat, laid seven affirmation cards in front of my mat (randomly chosen from several hundred I have hand-written), and turned on an Abraham-Hicks CD.

My practice felt great. I felt calm, happy, and energized. I'd done rag doll and five sun salutation A's when my iPhone rang. It was Philippe and the kids from Disney.

I smiled as I sat down on my mat to listen to their happy, high-vibration voices, with a joy and calm that wouldn't have been possible before I knew what I now know about creating the best life ever utilizing the three Practices.

Before I would've either: A. Not picked up the call (it was my practice time! And I was already "behind!"). Or B. Felt stressed and slightly annoyed during the phone call because "it was my practice time! And I was already behind!"

But I felt neither. All I felt was joy and a sense of "this moment is as it should be."

I continued to nest as I listened to adorable tales of pony rides, Mickey Mouse, Pluto, and Space Mountain, enjoying every moment.

When my kids announced that they had to go because it was time to take a dip in the pool at The Wilderness Lodge before heading back to The Magic Kingdom, I resumed my practice with a calm knowing that it didn't matter what time it was, my writing would get done, quickly and easily, at the perfect time.

Then when I did sit down to write, the words flowed easily, beautifully, and quickly as I continued to feel a sense of calm and joy.

This is what being in the flow feels like. This is what being in the Vortex of Creation feels like. And this is what you can create as you begin to mold your life, one moment at a time, exactly as you want it to be, utilizing the three Practices.

You can do this! How will you know you're on the right track or path? It's all about how you feel. If you feel great, you're on the path. If you feel stressed, you're not. If you feel inspired, on the path! Angry? Not. If you feel happy and calm, on the path. Jealous? Not. So in every moment, just check in: how am I feeling?

This is not about "how much have I accomplished? Am I on track with my work goals for today? Am I sticking to the schedule that I wrote out for myself?" This is about listening from within and trusting that a force that creates worlds will guide you and guide you well, so that things are created beautifully and easily. Let the Universe create it. It does a better job than we ever do.

# Chapter 77
# Now That Your Life Is Yours

"Every thought of yours is a real thing—a force."
- The Secret

PHOTO: TAYLOR WELLS

A few years ago Philippe and I were asked by the United Nations to be Yoga Peace Ambassadors. We were honored, said yes, and the night before we showed up at the UN to teach and be interviewed the interviewer emailed me 39 questions she was going to ask us during the interview. The 18th question read, "Now that your life is yours, what are your goals for your yoga?" Many of the previous questions had focused on Philippe and me leaving the rat race ten years ago to open our first Prana Power Yoga Studio so she was implying that our life is now "ours" since we left the rat race. An interesting concept. I agree, but not for the reasons you may be thinking.

My life is now "mine" because I have trained my mind, utilizing Deliberate Creation. This in concert with many years of a daily yoga practice and finding true and everlasting freedom around food by living the third Practice of creating the best life ever, has helped me train my mind to focus on the good in every situation. Every situation. There is always good if you train yourself to find it, and when you focus on the good for at least seventeen seconds, you change your vibration and draw to yourself more good because of The Law of Attraction.

So yes, my life is mine. Because I create it each and every moment by my focus.

You can too. Right now. In this moment. It don't matter what went down in the past. It don't matter if you work fourteen hour days in a corporate environment that you don't like. The environment don't matter, your thoughts do. And with time (and not a lot of time if you're focused), your environment will change too. With ease. To the best ever.

# Chapter 78
# The Play Date

The more often you practice, the more centered
and grounded you'll be and the sooner
you'll be living your best life ever.

My kids, now ages fourteen, eight, five, two, and two, have always loved play dates. The first year after I had my first child I wasn't really into play dates or playgroups. I was just soaking in and soaking up the whole Super-mom thang and had no desire to involve anyone else in my daughter's and my little world. Then when she turned one my higher self said, "It's time. Call in the one-year-olds!" And so I did, listening from within.

And oh how my daughter loved her play dates. She'd play with her friends for hours and enjoy every minute of it. This didn't stop as the years melted away like butter in a pan. With each passing year she loved play dates even more. When we would have our first play date with a new friend, the child's Super-mom would ask when she should pick up her child, suggesting an hour or so later. When I responded, "Oh, no, let's give 'em more time than that. Maybe pickup at dinner time?" the Super-mom was always surprised.

But those kids would play beautifully all day, for about seven hours or so, and require no intervention, no toys to speak of (unless you call a few sofa cushions a toy—they make a great fort), and very little food and water. In fact, I'd need to pop in every once in awhile to ask if they wanted anything to eat or drink, otherwise they'd go the whole play date without eating or drinking a thing.

My four other children have followed suit. It's so much fun to have their friends over because they all derive so much joy from just being together. They embody pure joy and creativity. Not from toys or me stepping in and suggesting a game or a movie or any other stimulus. From simply being together. It's quite beautiful to witness.

When did we lose this ability? When did we stop enjoying just being together, without the stimulation of food or alcohol or some sort of media? I'll tell you when. When we forgot who we are. When we lost touch with our center, with the essence of our being. These children are totally grounded in who they are so they don't need someone to define for them "what's fun" or what they "should" do. They follow their little Spirits and the time melts away, filled with joy and magic, as yours will too as you incorporate the three Practices. That's great news! With your newfound awareness and the three tools you're learning about in each chapter, you can reclaim this magic on a daily basis.

Sometimes people ask me how often they should practice yoga. I gently recommend that they practice yoga (Prana Power Yoga or the "yoga" of their choice) at least three times a week. The more often you practice, the more centered and grounded you'll be and the sooner you'll be living your best life ever. It's as simple as that.

So that's it! Cultivate and utilize the three Practices to create the best life ever and soon your days will fly by in what feels like a moment and you won't need all that "stuff" to "fill you up."

Reclaim your life and your world. As you want it. And when you get lost or confused (as we all do at times), breathe, believe, know that it's just contrast showing you what you do want in your life, and spend some time with children. They'll show you the way. They'll help you remember.

# Chapter 79
# Surrendering to The Flow

If it's taking time, it's getting
even better and more specific.

PHOTO: RAY MUCCI

As you incorporate the three Practices regularly, you'll notice your life improving dramatically and immediately. The law of Attraction is at work always and it doesn't discriminate or judge. It simply delivers what you put out to the Universe, immediately—unless there's resistance on your part.

You'll also notice that often things don't go exactly as you planned. Or as you planned at all. This is OK. This is good! This is the nature and the flow of the Universe. Our minds cannot conceive of the amazingly huge things that the Universe has in store for us. The Universe is creating and delivering on a totally different plane and frequency so it's gonna look a bit different. Or a lot different. But not different bad or worse, different great and better!

Your job? Practice the three Practices regularly and let go. Surrender to the process. Surrender to a force that creates miracles daily. A force that causes leaves to turn in the fall and the grass to grow in the spring.

I wrote this book in seven weeks, finishing four days before I had my twin sons. I was lined up to do so, so it flowed beautifully and easily. Not lined up by having twelve hours a day to write, mind you. I was living the day to day of having three kids and four yoga studios and building a restaurant. I was lined up energetically.

Then I had my twins and was so immersed in nursing every two hours, doing diaper free with them (also called "elimination communication"), and caring for my other three "big kids," that my book didn't cross my mind for about six months. When it did cross my mind I realized that it needed to be proofread and edited. And I would need a graphic designer for layout as well. So I began the search for the best editor, proofreader, and graphic designer ever and ended up choosing seven editors and proofreaders and one graphic designer from a pool of over a hundred who'd offered to help on yoga trade. Remember, we were putting every penny that came into Prana Power Yoga into our restaurant so I couldn't pay anyone with money at the time.

We went through the long process of editing, proof reading, and layout design and many months later my graphic designer sent me a hard copy of the manuscript for my final proofing. I spent thirty-five hours editing it and then left it in an airport on our way home from spring break in Aruba. This was in 2011.

When I realized what had happened, I sat for a moment on a window bench in Philippe's office, stunned, my mouth hanging open. After about a minute I realized that I had a choice. I could freak out or I could let it go right then and think about something else that made me happy. This is the essence of Deliberate Creation. I was deliberately creating by trusting that all would fall into place as it should and at the perfect time. I was trusting that "this moment is as it should be." Trusting that there was a reason that this had happened and all was well. I had no idea what the reason was but I let go and had faith, thanks to a lot of practice utilizing the three Practices.

After that I didn't have the heart or desire to look at my manuscript for a while. When my heart isn't into something I listen to this guidance because it's divine guidance in action. I only write and act from inspiration, an important part of Deliberately Creating. So I gently put my manuscript aside and focused on other things.

Less than three months after I lost my manuscript in the airport we were inspired to stop being a label, stop homeschooling, and sell our restaurant. Yeah, it bears repeating...good thing I lost my manuscript in that airport! This is a very different book than it would have been because the Universe has provided me with amazing clarity and wisdom about one of the keys to true freedom when creating the best life ever. I came to understand that the third Practice of creating the best life ever was different than I had originally believed. I understood from my life experience that the third Practice (for me) was total freedom to eat anything and everything that I want in moderation at all times. Without rules as to when and how and what. I noticed that with this newfound freedom I had even more energy than I'd had when I was raw vegan for seven years. I realized that what mattered more for me was my sense of freedom, not the nutritional content of the food I ate. I noticed that living without the label I still loved raw vegan foods and ate them frequently, and also loved other foods previously "forbidden."

The lesson? Ya never know exactly how or when it's coming—your wish, your dream, your miracle, your manifestation. But it's coming, if you utilize the three Practices regularly and you trust, surrender, and believe.

# Chapter 80
# Laugh. A Lot.

*"Laughter attracts joy, releases negativity,
and leads to miraculous cures."*
*- The Secret*

I laugh a lot. Mostly, what I laugh at are:

- Myself

- My kids

- Seinfeld DVDs

- Modern Family DVDs

Myself: Philippe and I had had a meeting at a big sporting company with whom we were exploring the potential of partnering. I'm usually the talker in meetings (no surprise there) and this meeting was no different. After the meeting as we were driving to pick up the twins at preschool, Philippe and I were laughing about my way with people. Philippe was imitating me and highlighting the fact that no matter where I am and with whom I'm talking, I go on and on about everything you've just read about in this book. He was imitating my voice and how I had all the VIP's in that meeting listening to everything I was saying even though I had moved the conversation quite far away from their agenda—and toward creating the best life ever. Talking with Philippe, I was laughing so hard that I was crying and it occurred to me—I'm laughing at myself. And I do so all the time! It's healthy to laugh, and to laugh at yourself. Best ever! So lighten up, laugh more, appreciate more, all is well.

My kids: My kids are a constant source of entertainment for Philippe and me. We keep a Google doc called "Best Family Quotes" and whenever any of our plus 5 say something that makes us laugh, we type it in. Notice and cherish those who makes you laugh. And spend more time around them. Laughing is a very high vibration.

Seinfeld DVD's: There's a reason why it was the most successful sitcom in history.

Modern Family DVD's: How can you not laugh with and adore Cam?

# Chapter 81
# Send Love, Light, and Gratitude to the Rascals

*"Send him some love and light every time you think about him, then drop it."*
*- Elizabeth Gilbert*

Every morning while I'm on cardio at the Y I take a few minutes to close my eyes and intentionally send love, light, and gratitude to everyone I can think of, and then to the world. Yes, even to the rascals who've hurt, betrayed, angered, or irritated me. Especially to the rascals! They are my biggest teachers, besides my five children. I acknowledge that I magnetized them into my life to teach me a lesson and ask the Universe and my higher self to give me wisdom, clarity, and guidance regarding the lesson.

When you send love, light, and gratitude out it comes back to you multiplied. Multiplied! But this ain't why Super-mom does it. I do it because it feels good. I do it because I wanna. I do it because it's my path.

To try this, intensify the feelings of love, light, and gratitude in your heart and then visualize it as a bright, sparkling, white light around your heart. Next see that glistening white light go out to those people you can see in your mind's eye—the family, the friends, the loved ones, the acquaintances, the colleagues, and yes, the rascals. All of 'em! Don't get into stories about the people, just send the energy out. The Law of Attraction matches the frequency you send out and returns it magnified.

If you do this regularly it will change your life and touch the lives of many.

# Chapter 82
# How To Clear Your Energy

Your energy is precious. Take good care of it.

Energy is where it's at. Energy is what makes you feel good, or not so good. Take care of your energy and stay connected with it. If it begins to drop, get negative or dark, clear it. The process is simple. Just follow these seven steps:

1. With your arms spread out wide say "With all my will and all my intent I bring in all my energy," and as you say this draw your arms in toward yourself as if you're giving yourself a hug. This "brings in all your energy."

2. With your hands above your head and your palms facing down say, "Higher self, clear all that needs to be cleared," as you press your palms down toward the earth flowing through all of your chakras.

3. Brush the tops of your fingertips against the area around your belly button (your third chakra, solar plexus) in a downward motion toward the earth (like brushing crumbs off your belly) and say, "I cut cords with the past."

4. Cover your third chakra with your hands and visualize something covering and protecting it, perhaps a thin film like Saran Wrap.

5. With your eyes closed visualize a bubble around you, which will protect your energy. Visualize it as a color—maybe white, silver, gold, or light pink. Whatever comes to you. It may change daily.

6. Visualize your entire body filling up with golden white light from the bottom of your feet to the top of your head.

7. Visualize and make a hand gesture that mimics "zipping up" the front of your body, thereby "zipping out" out all negative energy.

# Chapter 83
# How to Shield Your Chakras

It's important to keep your energy clean and clear. One way that our energy is messed with is when people "suck you dry" with their energy or intention. Usually they aren't even aware that they're doing it, poor loves. Also, sometimes "situations" or environments drain our energy.

This is why it's important to know how to clear your energy and keep it clear by shielding a few chakras that are sometimes drained by "energy vampires," environments, or situations.

Just follow these five easy steps:

1. Every morning when you wake up, before you get out of bed, thank the Universe for all that you are grateful for.

2. Close your eyes and visualize your second chakra open, like a flower. Perhaps use your hands to mimic an open flower. See the flower (maybe a daisy or any flower with petals—whatever you like) and see its color and texture. The color and texture may change daily.

3. See the open flower (chakra) closing, perhaps using your hands to mimic a flower closing its petals. Once it's "closed," that chakra is shielded.

4. Move to the third chakra (solar plexus) and repeat steps two and three.

5. Move to your heart chakra and do almost the same things described in steps two and three, except don't close it. See it open and beautiful.

# The Begininning
# Part 2

PHOTO: MEGAN GEORGE

So now you have it. You have it! You have the three Practices—the keys to the best life ever. So go out and create whatever you desire. And have fun in the process. Remember, it's all about joy.

You can do this, and you will. When you feel out of sorts, off track, or off the path, no worries. Breathe in and breathe out, pick up this book again, and read a chapter—any chapter. Or maybe even just a few lines of a chapter. It'll put you back on track in a heartbeat.

Remember that it's what you do most of the time that matters and there's no such thing as perfect.

I'm excited for this new beginning for you.

Have the best day and the best life ever!

Namaste!

Taylor plus 5

P.S. Thanks for reading my book. I had a blast writing it or I wouldn't have done it since I practice Deliberate Creation all day every day. Another book is on the way! In the meantime, check out my blogs and websites:

*Pranapoweryoga.com

*Super-mom.com

*Bostonherald.com ("Best Life Ever" in the Lifestyle Blogs Section)

*Vitacost.com ("Best Life Ever")

*Momonomics.com (My blogs are posted on Mondays and Wednesdays.)

# About Taylor

Taylor is a happy Super-mom of five; Activist; Author; Boston Herald Blogger and Columnist; Clinical Psychologist; Co-creator, Co-founder, Co-owner, and Co-director of Prana Power Yoga (Brooklyn, New York; Cambridge, Massachusetts; Newton, Massachusetts; Union Square, New York; and Winchester, Massachusetts); Co-creator of The Prana Cleanse™; Consultant; Creator and sole writer of Super-mom.com; Master Yoga Teacher; Momonomics.com blogger; Reiki Master; United Nations Yoga Peace Ambassador; and Vitacost.com blogger.

At age thirteen Taylor lived with her tennis coach Nick Bollettieri in Sarasota, Florida to train to go pro. It was a year of intense discipline, focus, and many lessons. Thanks to her year at Nick's Taylor learned the importance of both discipline and balance since her life at Nick's had an incredible amount of discipline but very little balance. Seeking balance, she returned to Calabasas, California after a year of training with Nick where she played #1 singles on her high school tennis team and USTA tournaments, went to parties and football games, and was honored to be voted Homecoming Queen by her peers in her senior year.

Taylor studied to be a journalist during her undergraduate years at Brown University and went on to study and train to be a clinical psychologist at Columbia University, Massachusetts School of Professional Psychology, and Harvard University. Her clinical psychology training is useful on her path as she helps thousands of people remember who they are, unlock their pure potential, and create their best life ever.

Taylor transformed her body, mind, and life with her yoga practice and knew intuitively after her first practice that it was her dharma to spread the Prana and the light of yoga to others. Taylor and her husband Philippe left the rat race in 2002 to open their first Prana Power Yoga in Newton, Massachusetts. Now with all of the freedom and abundance that Prana, the Universe, and the three Practices have brought them, they continue to create their best lives ever.

Taylor learns a lot every day on her mat, from her yoga students, and from the many adventures and lessons that the Universe sends her way; however, her biggest teachers are her five children, Madison (14), Sagey (8), Phoenix (5), Dakota (2), and Montana (2).